COLLECTIBLE

Cups & Saucers

Jim & Susan Harran

COLLECTOR BOOKS

A Division of Schroeder Publishing Co., Inc.

The current values in this book should be used only as a guide. They are not intended to set prices, which vary from one section of the country to another. Auction prices as well as dealer prices vary greatly and are affected by condition and demand. Neither the Authors nor the Publisher assumes responsibility for any losses which might be incurred as a result of consulting this guide.

Searching For A Publisher?

We are always looking for knowledgeable people considered experts within their fields. If you feel that there is a real need for a book on your collectible subject and have a large comprehensive collection, contact Collector Books.

ON THE COVER

Teacup and saucer by Paragon China Co., c. 1939 – 1949, $40.00 – 60.00.

Cover design: Beth Summers
Book layout: Karen Geary

Printed in the U.S.A. by Image Graphics, Paducah, KY

CONTENTS

DEDICATION

In loving memory of Esther and Gilbert Pitzl
and Anna and Hugh Harran.

ABOUT THE AUTHORS

Susan and Jim Harran, antique dealers for 15 years, specialize in English and continental porcelains. The Harrans write feature articles for various antique publications and have a monthly column in *Antique Week*, entitled "The World of Ceramics." Susan is a member of the Antique Appraisal Association of America Inc. The Harrans enjoy traveling around the country to keep abreast of trends in the antiques market place. They reside in Neptune, New Jersey.

ACKNOWLEDGMENTS

We would like to express our appreciation to several collectors who so generously gave of their time and knowledge to make this book a reality. A special thank you to Beth and Ron Prielipp of Salina, Kansas, who were willing to share their collection of Irish and American Belleek cups and saucers, sending us over thirty pictures photographed by their friend, Jean Kozubowski, from Lindsborg, Kansas.

We would like to thank Marguerite Verley of New Lenox, Illinois. Marguerite, who is writing a book on British tableware, shared her extensive knowledge of early British cups and saucers with us, as well as some lovely photographs from her collection.

We are indebted to Linda and Richard Gibbs for their hospitality in allowing us to visit their home in New Jersey and photograph their spectacular collection of miniature cups and saucers. Because of their generosity, we were able to photograph over sixty cups and saucers for our book.

Special thanks also to Gerri Robbins, owner of Robbins Rarities Ltd, from Manlius, New York; Linda H. Richard from Bryan, Texas; and Don Erlenbush from Altamont, Illinois, for contributing photographs of cups and saucers from their collections. We appreciate the time spent photographing and researching them.

Thanks to Todd Robertson, owner of Shore Service Photo in Neptune City, New Jersey, and his staff for their patience and help with our challenging task of photographing over 400 cups and saucers.

Lastly, we thank all those individuals who allowed us to photograph their cups and saucers at antique shows and shops. They graciously gave us permission to come into their booths, often disrupting and rearranging their displays. Without the following dealers' assistance, we would have been unable to complete our book:

     Roz and Jeff Abrams, White Plains, MD
     Antiques Showcase at the Black Horse, Denver, PA
     Jan and Don Applegate, Jan's Delightful Debris, NJ
     Patrick Cerra, Etruria, Plainfield, NH
     Ronnie Evans Antiques, Enterprise, AL
     Timothy Green, Alexandria, VA
     Terri and Phil Harlan, Deer Chase Antiques, Boca Raton, FL
     Margo Hasson, Golden Age Antiques, CT
     Barbara K. Hegedus Antiques, PA
     Jan-Tiques, Hamden, CT
     M & M Antiques, Egg Harbor, NJ
     M.T.E. Antiques, Norwalk, CT
     Laura Messinger and Regina Negrotti, Tablescapes, Trenton, NJ
     Noble Peddler, Torrington, CT
     Michael Raulston and Ted Birbilis, Roadside Antiques, Dallas, TX
     Judith Ravnitzky, Mahopac, NY
     Robert Schicke, Reclaimed Memories, Rockaway, NJ
     Joan and John Senkewicz, J's Antiques and Collectibles, New Monmouth, NJ

PREFACE

As antique dealers for fifteen years, we specialize in fine continental and English porcelains. A few years ago, we began buying and selling antique cups and saucers and found them to be fascinating. An infinite variety of cups and saucers are available for both the new and experienced collector, and they can be found in all price ranges. There is probably no better way to thoroughly know and understand the various ceramic manufacturers than to study cups and saucers.

We were surprised to find that, other than Michael Berthoud's *A Compendium of British Cups*, there are no other books in print available on cups and saucers, specifically. In order to fairly price our merchandise, it has been necessary to dig through general price guides and auction catalogs, as well as to observe the prices on similar pieces at shows and shops, to try to ferret out realistic prices to charge. Many of our customers have asked us if there was a resource available to help them learn about cups and saucers.

We realized there was a need for a book about collectible cups and saucers and decided to write one. It has taken us two years to research this vast field. Our purpose has been to concentrate on actual cups and saucers that are readily available in the marketplace, rather than museum pieces; therefore, all but one photograph in the book were taken from cups and saucers that have been in our inventory or that of other dealers at antique shows, shops, or from private collections.

Our purpose in this book is to provide, all in one source, information on the history of tea, coffee, and hot chocolate, early cup and saucer forms and shapes, and how cups and saucers were made and decorated. We include a brief history on the most popular manufacturers, a representative sample of their production, and what, we hope, is a realistic price range, and some helpful information for collectors.

We have divided the book into six collecting categories, although they overlap, and many collectors enjoy examples from each. The first group is a representative collection of early cups and saucers dating from the 1700s until 1875.

The second group, dedicated to the advanced collector, is cabinet cups — those exquisite works of art that were too fragile and costly to be used. Because true cabinet cups and saucers are so rare and usually found only in museums, we have taken the liberty to include cups and saucers that we think are especially fine, even though we know they were once part of a tea or coffee set and made to be used.

The third category, late nineteenth and twentieth century dinnerware, is by far the largest and the foundation of most collections. In this group we have included the ever-popular dinner, demitasse, and chocolate cups and saucers from companies in Europe, England, Japan, and the United States.

A fourth group that is growing in popularity is the lovely twentieth century English bone china and pottery cups and saucers. They are abundant, and the prices are reasonable, making them perfect for the beginner to collect. We also discuss the Shelley and Chintz phenomena.

The fifth popular category is miniatures. Although these tiny gems were made as early as the seventeenth century, they are as elusive to find as "a needle in the haystack," and prices are soaring.

Cups and saucers from our sixth group, figurals, are also difficult to find. Alas, we were only able to find a small number to photograph! Perhaps their scarcity is one reason why collectors search for these whimsical treasures.

There are several other mediums or cup forms that we have not addressed in this book, simply because we had to draw the line somewhere. An entire book could be written about glass cups and saucers. Examples of American cut glass of the brilliant period and exquisitely enameled glass are eagerly collected today. A few other popular collectibles are mustache cups, mugs, Japanese lithophanes, and souvenir and coronation cups and saucers.

Many publications supplied helpful information, and these sources are acknowledged in the Bibliography. Hopefully, this book will make it easier for the beginning, as well as the advanced collector, dealer, and appraiser, to identify and price cups and saucers. We realize that in a book of this nature and scope, some degree of error is unavoidable, and we apologize in advance.

We would appreciate hearing your comments, and our address is below:

Susan and Jim Harran
208 Hemlock Drive
Neptune, NJ 07753

If you would like a reply, please include a self-addressed stamped envelope.

EARLY DEVELOPMENT

THE HISTORY OF TEA

Legend has it that a tea leaf was discovered in China 3,000 years ago, when Emperor Shan-Nung was boiling his drinking water to purify it, and some leaves from a nearby tree were blown into the pot, imparting a delicate flavor. From that point on, the Emperor ordered the tea leaves to be put in his water all the time.

In India the discovery is credited to Darma, a Buddist priest in the first century, who vowed to spend seven years in sleepless meditation. Becoming drowsy after five years, he chewed a few tea leaves and immediately became invigorated and was able to complete his vows.

The ships of the East India Company had begun regular sailings to China in the 1600s and introduced the exotic drink of tea to Europe. Much of the appeal of tea drinking was the result of the attraction of the strange equipment it required. Delicate blue and white porcelain teapots and tea bowls were also brought over from China. This lovely china became a status symbol, and tea drinking provided an opportunity for people to show off their wealth with glamorous imported china. In 1660, Samuel Pepys wrote in his diary, "I did send for a cup of tea, a China drink, of which I had never drunk before."

THE HISTORY OF COFFEE

It is believed the coffee plant was discovered about 1,000 years ago in Ethiopia. A shepherd, noticing his sheep were acting lively at night and not sleeping much, spent a few nights observing their behavior. The shepherd noticed the sheep were eagerly eating the blossoms and fruit of a plant he had never noticed before. Trying the food himself, the shepherd became so animated, his friends thought he was drunk. When he told them of his discovery, they all agreed it was a gift of God and should be enjoyed.

Coffee has been brewed since the fifteenth century in Arabia, often keeping monks awake during their long prayer services. The priests believed the coffee was like liquor and tried to forbid it, but the coffee habit spread all over Arabia and neighboring countries.

By the early sixteenth century Turkish merchants transported coffee from Arabia to Constantinople, and it got to Europe about 1585, when Venetian traders brought it to Italy. The first coffeehouses were opened in Venice in the seventeenth century, and the drink reached England in 1637. The drink spread to the rest of Europe where it found much resistance from government and religious leaders. It was forbidden in Sweden, and in Germany a special license was required for anyone who wanted to roast coffee. In the early 1600s Captain John Smith is said to have introduced coffee into Virginia.

THE HISTORY OF HOT CHOCOLATE

South American Indians have grown cocoa trees for over 1,000 years. It is said the Aztec Indians valued the cocoa bean so much that they used it both as a drink and as a unit of currency.

Columbus was said to have brought a few beans back to Spain after his voyage to South America in 1498. Soon Spanish explorers began to export cocoa beans to Spain and other European countries. Factories were built to make a drinking chocolate, and by the middle of the seventeenth century, the drink had spread throughout western Europe.

THE FORMS

Cups designed specifically for coffee, chocolate, or tea began to appear in Europe in the seventeenth century. These drinks were quite expensive, and the earliest cups were made of silver for the wealthy. The use of silver was impractical, however, because the hot liquid made the cup too hot to handle. As the quality of ceramics improved in the eighteenth century, silver cups declined, and examples are rare.

Throughout Europe and England in the 1700s, there were thousands of coffee and chocolate houses where people could gather to discuss the news of the day. Coffeehouses had a number of other uses, serving as political meeting houses, marriage bureaus, insurance offices, early post offices, and gaming houses. In England the renowned Lloyd's of London Insurance Company got its start inside a coffeehouse. In the United States at the Merchants Coffeehouse in New York in 1738, it is said that plans for the American Revolution were discussed.

A number of pleasure gardens were also available where the customers could sit and watch the passing parade of fashionable society, drinking tea and listening to music in the open air. Neither the public tea gardens nor the rowdier coffeehouses would have wished to provide expensive silver or Oriental porcelain for their customers, only to have it cracked or broken; therefore, these early mugs and cups were made out of stoneware and earthenware.

The growth in popularity of tea and coffee drinking for use in the home and its eventual availability for the common man created an entirely new business for the pottery industry throughout the world.

TEA BOWLS AND CUPS

The earliest utensils for tea drinking were small porcelain and stoneware bowls imported from China by the East Indian Company in the early seventeenth century. European and English tea bowls, imitating Chinese and Japanese originals, were produced in stoneware, earthenware, and porcelain from the early eighteenth century onward and were often decorated with "chinoiserie" or Chinese-type motifs.

In use, the tea bowl presented a problem, especially when the bowl was as small as the early ones. The bowl became very hot and could only be held by the finger and thumb by grasping the top rim or foot rim. The thumb could be placed under the foot and the finger on the rim, but it couldn't be set down in this position. For those drinkers with steady hands, it could be taken to the mouth on the saucer. Tea bowls did not present a problem for the Chinese as they drank their tea lukewarm.

In the eighteenth century the rather rare handled teacups were, as a rule, only supplied with expensive tea sets. By about 1810 handles were fitted to the bowl to form the now familiar teacup, and this form became almost universal.

COFFEE CANS AND CUPS

Coffee in England and on the continent was often served in a can — a straight-sided cylinder with a handle jutting out at the right. It measured 2½" high and 2½" in diameter. The saucers were indented and called stands. Such coffee cans became fashionable in the second half of the eighteenth century up to 1820. After that time, the coffee can gave way to the more fanciful form of the coffee cup.

A coffee cup is normally tall and narrow in comparison to a teacup and has one handle. Although called coffee cups, they could be used for tea as well.

The demitasse cup originated in France and means half a cup. These smaller coffee cups were used to drink the stronger espresso-type coffee after a meal. Early demitasse cups and saucers were often exquisitely decorated and part of cabaret or déjeuner sets.

SAUCERS

Saucers in their present form evolved out of the Oriental saucer-dish, with its slightly upward curving sides and central depression and the teacup stand, originally a simple circular stand with an indentation in the center to hold the cup steady. With its high sides, the saucer-dish was often regarded as no more than a shallow tea bowl, whose greater surface area allowed more rapid cooling of the liquid; thus, the early custom of drinking tea from the saucer rather than the cup. As teacups became larger, the saucers gradually shrunk in size.

FULL SERVICE

A full tea and coffee set in the eighteenth century might consist of:

teapot and cover	waste bowl
teapot stand	spoon tray
tea canister and cover	2 saucer-like plates or stands
coffeepot and cover	12 tea bowls
sugar bowl and cover	6, 8, or 12 coffee cans
milk or cream jug, some with covers	12 saucers

One of the reasons many cups, cans, and bowls are found today without saucers is because only 12 saucers came in the typical teaset, and they were used interchangeably with the can, cup, or bowl. A tea bowl/cup, coffee can/cup, and saucer is referred to as a trio.

CHOCOLATE CUPS

Hot chocolate was a very popular drink in the eighteenth century, particularly in France, and many cups had a dual function. By the 1760s chocolate cups tended to be larger and taller than a coffee cup, sometimes with two handles and a cover.

CUP PLATES

In days when handleless tea bowls were used, it was fashionable, as well as more practical, to pour the hot liquid into the deep saucer and drink from it. While this polite saucer sipping was going on, the cup was rested in a special cup plate, a little flat dish about three or four inches in diameter. The first cup plates were made of earthenware pottery. In the United States glass cup plates were often favored. By 1840, cup plates were no longer in style.

BREAKFAST CUPS

These large cups held two regular-sized cups of coffee or tea and were often included in a full tea service.

SHAPES

1750–1800

Early shapes were often quite plain with simple lines. Many cups were molded into lovely floral or fruit forms. Vertical fluting became popular, and Meissen's Royal Flute shape was introduced in 1775. Coffee cups were straight sided, and the bucket-shaped can was developed in 1790. Early tea bowls had straight foot rims. Loop handles were common, some with inner spurs, others with Chinese-style flattened thumb rests. In France curved ear-shaped handles were popular on Old Paris cups. Sevres coffee cans had the much copied kicked loop handle.

1800–1815

By 1800, the dominant shape was the Royal Flute, scalloped and waisted with a kicked loop handle. The plain, rounded Bute shape was introduced with a plain loop or ring handle. The squat slightly flared rimmed Porriger shape was popular in England. The square French handle was developed in 1800. The lemon-shaped cup with pulled up handle was developed in Berlin about 1800 and was called the Campaner shape. Tea bowls had more rounded footrims.

1815–1845

By the 1820s, the influence of the romantic movement began to affect all aspects of interior design. The ladies who swooned over Lord Bryon's poems wanted more flamboyant tewares. The dominant cup shape, the London shape, was introduced in 1812, and it remained popular until 1830. Fluted cups of many styles with coiled, French loop, broken loop, old English, and "D" shaped handles were in vogue. The Adelaide shape was introduced in 1835 and the footed Glasgow shape in 1845. Gadrooning, often used in silver designs, was popular. This decorative series of curved, inverted flutings, somewhat like a clenched fist, was used on a variety of shapes.

1845–1875

Waisted cups with divided handles, sometimes with leaf terminals were fashionable. Deep footed or pedestal cups were popular. Straight-lined and tapered cups were in evidence. Oval ring, loop, and rope handles were in style.

1875–Present

This period saw the beginnings of the Art Nouveau movement that spread across the United States, England, and the Continent. The movement was characterized by flowing, sensuous lines, swirling leaf and floral forms, and other naturalistic motifs. Cups were made in the shape of molded flowers and leaves, often with twig handles and feet or shaped like a coral branch.

In 1896, Joseph Shelley introduced his famous Dainty White six-flute shape, and the next fifty years produced other delicate, fluted shapes. The Art Deco movement of the 1920s and 1930s produced angular shapes and handles, such as the Vogue and Mode shapes.

Although a large factory might have produced hundreds of new patterns each year, shapes are used repeatedly because of the enormous expense of introducing a new shape.

THE MANUFACTURING PROCESS

There are two basic methods of taking a shapeless lump of clay and making it into an object of beauty and usefulness like a cup or saucer. Throwing is one method, and molding is another.

THROWING

The throwing method is certainly not for mass producing an item, but it has a kind of charm. In the throwing method, a portion of clay is centered on the potter's wheel, and as it rotates, the potter skillfully shapes it with his hands to the desired form and shape. It has that one-of-a-kind personal touch that is not possible in mass production.

MOLDING

Molding is ideal for long production runs of objects which have to be identical in form and size and for intricate shapes. When cakes of clay paste are obtained in a workable state, they are ready for one of three methods of molding: jiggering, jollying, or casting.

In jiggering, a disk of clay is placed on a rotating plaster head, and a template is pressed against it, forming the shape. In making a saucer, for example, the plastic head forms the face of the saucer, and the template forms the bottom. The paste rotates as on the potter's wheel, but the mold and template form the shape.

Jollying is a process very similar to jiggering. The piece is formed through rotation. A mold and template are used. The plaster mold determines the shape of the piece. In a cup, for example, the template forms its inner surface.

Casting is used for the production of all pieces that can be neither jiggered nor jollied due to their special shape. Liquid paste or slip is poured into the plaster mold, the inner surface of which is the shape of the piece to be cast, until it is completely filled. The plaster mold absorbs water from the slip. Then the porcelain paste is formed in the desired shape. As the paste hardens, it will shrink slightly and is easily removed from the mold.

After any one of the three processes is completed, the piece is trimmed and sponged to a smooth finish. If assembly of the pieces is required, for instance a handle to a cup, this is accomplished by using slip to attach it to the cup form.

The names of these methods may differ with a particular manufacturer, although the process is basically the same.

DESIGNING AND MODELING

To create a new shape, the designer must first draw each item and establish a design. A mold must then be made before a piece of fine porcelain can be produced. The modeler must bear in mind that there will be a reduction in size during the bisque firing, so the model must be at least six percent larger than the finished item. The mold is usually made of plaster of Paris or a resin material.

Cups and saucers are actually produced from working molds. These molds are an exact copy in the reverse of the original model. Molds must be very dry before they are used, so that the dry plaster wall will quickly absorb moisture from the paste. To produce a single item in large quantities, many working molds may be required as the molds wear out. In a cup and saucer, a working mold is required for the shape of the cup itself, another mold for the handle, and one for the saucer. Slip is used for the adhesive. Making these separate working molds is a true art requiring great skill. Model and mold making is one of the most important parts of the production process.

BISQUE FIRING

The first firing of a piece is called bisque or biscuit and requires very careful handling. The molded piece goes into a kiln. It takes a piece about 30 hours of firing, and the piece will reach temperatures as high as 1,750° Fahrenheit. After cooling to room temperature, it is ready for further processing.

GLAZE

The glaze applied to a cup and saucer serves several purposes. First, to form a completely impenetrable surface; secondly, to provide durability to the items for long and hard usage; and lastly, to produce the translucency which is characteristic of a fine porcelain cup and saucer.

Quartz, feldspar, chalk, and dolomite are mixed together to make a creamy liquid called glaze. The ingredients may vary slightly from company to company for the desired effect.

Glaze is applied to a cup or saucer by dipping it in a vat of the liquid. The bisque piece is very absorbent, and a layer of glaze is built up. The glaze must be of just the right thickness.

FIRING

After the glaze has been applied, the piece is again put in a kiln. When the proper temperature of 2,600° Fahrenheit is reached, the glaze melts, covering the piece with a shiny finish. At the same time, complete vitrification of the body and its translucency is achieved.

When all the processes have been completed, with some minor variations, depending on the specific manufacturer and the period, we have a beautiful finished cup and saucer ready for decoration.

DECORATION

MOLDED DESIGNS

The early forms of decoration were often simple molded designs or intricate relief decoration like the ones achieved by the Meissen Company in their famous Swan Service. Sprig-molded ornamentation derived from Chinese porcelain occurred on early English porcelain as well.

UNDERGLAZE BLUE

Most factories in the early days depended on the production of tea wares decorated in underglaze blue in order to compete with Chinese exports. Blue, made from cobalt, was the only color which could withstand the high temperatures in which the glaze was fired. If other colors were wanted, they had to be added after the glaze was fired.

POLYCHROME ENAMELS

Johann Höroldt, manager of the Meissen Company in the 1720s, developed 16 new enamel paints which are still the basic paints for porcelain decoration today. His contributions made Meissen a leader of polychrome enamel painting, and his unique style is still being used. In contrast to the blue and white ware, the shapes of early polychromed enameled porcelain tea bowls and saucers are much simpler, relying entirely on the effect of the pale, glowing colors of the enamels, highlighted by gilding.

During the mid-eighteenth century, Oriental scenes were very popular. Meissen created the well-known "chinoiseries" or Chinese-type designs, and these were used by many English factories. The Japanese Kakiemon style had influence on many companies as well. The richly decorated Imari-style patterns of Coalport and Derby stand out with areas of deep underglaze blue with overglaze red, green, and gilt. This style was cheap to produce because the repetitive designs could be painted by apprentices, and yet it looked ornate and rich.

HAND PAINTING

Hand painting was the favored method of decoration on the elegant teaware commissioned by the wealthy and titled classes. Tiny sprigs of flowers, swags of leaves, and garlands of rose buds and exotic birds were some of the lovely designs on porcelain cups and saucers of the eighteenth century. Many designs were richly gilded. Toward the end of the eighteenth century a new fashion in decoration was introduced to the world of elegant teaware for which Derby porcelain was largely responsible. Scenic and landscape painting of a very high quality was produced, and an amazing "wash" effect similar to a watercolor painting was created.

TRANSFER PRINTING

Printing was introduced in the 1750s to achieve a high level of detail and accuracy as well as the ability to produce a high volume of items with identical patterns at a relatively low cost. A designer would create a pattern that would be pleasing to the eye, as well as suitable for placing on a variety of shapes, such as a saucer, small tea bowl, or narrow coffee cup. Once the design was put on paper and approved by the head of the factory, the design would be transferred on to a copper plate. This was most likely done by piercing a series of small holes through the paper to outline the main details of the pattern. The paper was then laid on the copper plate, and a fine powder was sprinkled on the surface to mark the plate. The image was then engraved into the plate by a sharp instrument. The preliminary design was then improved by further cutting and the use of acid. Once a plate was engraved, hundreds of articles could be decorated with the design.

At the Worcester Company painting over a printed outline was developed in 1770. Semi-skilled painters could fill in the outline at a fraction of the cost of skilled freehand painting.

Around 1800 another method of engraving, bat printing, was used on many English ceramics with good results. The design was transferred from the copper plate to the glazed article by a bat of glue and another substance. The copper plate was charged with an oily substance, the gluey bat transferred to the article, and powdered color was then dusted over the article to adhere to the oiled parts.

GILDING

Gold ornamentation has been used to enhance fine porcelains since the early Oriental teawares imported into England and the continent in the seventeenth century. Early methods were japanned gilding and oil gilding.

Japanned gilding was used from 1740 on English soft paste porcelain. Fine gold leaf was applied to the glaze with a mixture of other chemicals and then fired in a small oven. It was then protected by a piece of thin paper and burnished or polished with a hardstone, such as an agate.

Oil gilding was not as durable or as brilliant. An adhesive mixture was painted on the rims and patterns of the piece and left to dry. After three days this gold leaf was cut to match the pattern and pressed on to the piece. It was then fired at a very low temperature.

Honey gilding was introduced in France and was first used in the early 1700s. The powdered gold was mixed with honey before being painted with a brush on to the glazed ware. After firing at a low temperature, it was burnished and could even be chased with a tool. Although duller than japanned gilding, it was much more durable.

In about 1785 honey gilding gave way to mercury gilding. Powdered gold was added to a mercury mixture which vaporized when heated, leaving a film of dull gold which was then vigorously burnished.

Acid gilding was introduced at Minton in 1865 and was later used by most of the leading factories. The pleasing contrast between matt and shiny gold is achieved by use of an acid. The parts to be left matt are recessed by acid so that when gold is applied, the raised surface only was burnished, leaving the gold dull and matt where the design had been etched into the surface of the item.

Collectors treasure cups and saucers that are decorated with gilding. Many French Limoges firms used gilt on the rims of cups and saucers and on the handles. The use of dotted gilt decoration on the sides of cup handles originated in 1800 at Worcester and Grainger.

LUSTER

Luster decoration, imitating silver, copper, or gold, was used in Great Britain, as well as Germany, especially on teaware. The luster is achieved by applying a thin metallic film to earthenware or porcelain. Silver luster was derived from a platinum film rather than silver which tarnishes. Where a gold film is used, the luster will be a pleasing pink tint. The bat-printed cups and saucers of the mid-nineteenth century with luster decoration or trim are still plentiful and reasonably priced.

EARLY MANUFACTURERS

CHINESE EXPORT PORCELAIN

The lovely teaware, decorated in underglaze blue, brought over by the East India Company to England and Europe from China was immediately successful. By the eighteenth century the demand for Chinese export porcelain became widespread. Canton blue and white dinnerware was popular, as well as export wares in the famille rose palette. Especially sought after by collectors are the cups and saucers of the "rose medallion" pattern which contains reserves of birds, flowers, and figures in shades of pink and green.

MEISSEN COMPANY

The first European porcelain company was founded in Meissen, Germany, in 1710, and was called the Royal Saxon Porcelain Manufactory. Although the Chinese had been using hard paste porcelain for a long time, the development of porcelain in Europe was the result of a collaboration of three people: physicist Walther von Tschirnausen, alchemist Johann Frederick Böttger, and their patron, Augustus the Strong, Elector of Saxony.

The porcelain was very plastic and could be molded into many intricate designs, especially on the borders of plates and saucers. One of the most elaborate early dinnerware sets was the "Swan Service" ordered by Count Bruhl in 1737. It included 2,000 pieces, and the entire surface was modeled in low relief with animals and water plants. The Meissen Company still makes pulls of this set for customers today.

Pastoral scenes were popular in the 1730s, and the French painter Watteau was frequently copied. A cup and saucer from the "green Watteau" pattern is highly prized.

During the mid-eighteenth century, Oriental scenes were favored by the court, and teaware was created with the well-known chinoiserie designs, as well as the Japanese dragon patterns. Early tea bowls can be found in these styles, often with gilt scrollwork and footrims.

THE ENGLISH POTTERS

When the Grand Union Canal was completed in Great Britain in 1772, the cost of transport fell dramatically. It became possible for thousands of ordinary households in England to replace their pewter and silver cups and horn mugs with china tableware. The growth in popularity of tea drinking created an entire new business for the pottery industry at Stoke-on-Trent in Staffordshire and throughout England.

BOW CHINA WORKS

Bow China Works is probably the earliest of the English porcelain factories. In Defoe's *Tour of Great Britain* written in 1748 he observed, "The first village we come to is Bow where a large manufactory of porcelain is lately set-up. They have already made large quantities of cups,

16

saucers, etc., which by some skillful persons are said to be little inferior to those which were brought from China." Bow made teaware in blue and white decorated in the Oriental style.

CHELSEA PORCELAIN WORKS

By 1745, the Chelsea factory produced the first successful English soft paste porcelain and was one of the most famous of all English porcelain factories. Their teaware was the most richly decorated of eighteenth century English ceramics. They often imitated the delicate coloring and restrained shapes of Meissen tableware. A teabowl from Chelsea would be a rare find today.

JOSIAH WEDGWOOD

Ten tons of coal were required to fire one ton of clay in a pottery kiln. Firing to a lower temperature used less coal. Earthenware was, therefore, cheaper to make than the higher fired stoneware pottery. In 1760 Josiah Wedgwood produced the first commercially successful earthenware which was pale enough to resemble porcelain. It was named creamware and has been called Britain's great contribution in the history of ceramics. It could be painted or printed like porcelain, usually after glazing. Queen Charlotte was so pleased with the ware she allowed it to be called Queen's ware.

Perhaps the most famous dinner service in the world was the 952-piece creamware set produced by Wedgwood for the Empress Catherine of Russia in 1773–74. It was decorated with 1,244 views of scenic Great Britain.

Because of archaeological discoveries in Pompeii in the 1770s, the decoration of the ancient Greeks and Romans became fashionable. In the spirit of this neoclassic style, the ideal material for teaware was a pottery with little or no glaze covering it. This would show the fine detail of molded or applied reliefs without hiding it under a thick layer of glaze. In 1767, Josiah Wedgwood developed basalt, an unglazed black stoneware made from native clay, ironstone, manganese, and ochre. He also made red stoneware teaware, as well as his famous and eagerly collected jasperware with classical scenes in bas-relief.

JOSIAH SPODE

Josiah Spode II (1754–1827) is credited with the discovery of bone china. Bone ash is combined with china clay, thus giving it more stability. By 1800, other factories were adding bone ash to china clay as well. This became the standard English porcelain body throughout the nineteenth century and remains popular today. The light weight and translucency of bone china makes it appealing for teaware. It has been said that if you hold a teacup up to the light and can see the shadow from your hand through it, it is bone china.

MINTON

In 1793, Thomas Minton, with two other partners, opened a pottery in Stoke-on-Trent. For the first few years blue-printed earthenwares were made similar to those made by other companies in the area. In 1798 cream-colored earthenware and bone china were introduced, greatly increasing the sales of the company. During this early period, production was concentrated on table, tea, and dessert wares. Surviving pattern books show a great variety of printed, enamel painted, and gilded designs. Subjects were landscapes, chinoiseries, French-inspired floral patterns, lustres, and neoclassical designs. In her charming book, *A Cup of Tea*, Geraldene Holt includes many lovely watercolor paintings of early teabowls and saucers, taken from an early Minton pattern book. Some of the patterns are quite ornate and complicated; others are beautiful in their simplicity.

MASON, CHARLES JAMES & CO.

The Mason brothers, who operated one of the most successful nineteenth century Staffordshire potteries, began to produce a brightly colored, extremely durable range of teawares in a heavy, faintly transparent earthenware with a metallic ring. They patented it in 1813 as Ironstone China, and it was instantly successful. Patterns were based on the richly gilded bright colored Japanese designs popular at the time.

THE UNITED STATES

In the eighteenth century, it was almost impossible to find American china fine enough to decorate the home. Although potteries had sprung up all over the United States, they produced utilitarian wares such as redware, stoneware and yellow ware almost exclusively. Buyers looked to China and Europe for their fine porcelain.

William Ellis Tucker opened a porcelain factory in Philadelphia in 1826. At first, decorative and useful Queen's ware was made in the classical shapes of the Empire style. Many designs were copied from English and French porcelains. Tucker was the first company to use American subject matter on porcelain, and his designs included historical views and patriotic heroes. Many pieces were unmarked to resemble unmarked French porcelains.

Tea bowl and saucer (miniature).

Unmarked, possibly Chinese, late eighteenth century.

Slightly flared bowl with simple underglaze blue decoration and overglaze enamels.

$200.00 – 250.00.

Teacup without saucer.

Meissen Marcolini period, c. 1745–1817.

Early cup with blue underglaze painting in chinoiserie motif.

$75.00 – 95.00.

Another view of Meissen cup showing mark.

Coffee cup and saucer.

Meissen, c. 1860–1875.

Shell motif in relief, pearlized pink and white on pale green, gold embellishment; gold band inside rim of cup very worn.

$100.00–125.00.

Tea bowl and saucer (miniature).

J. G. Paulus, Bohemia, c. 1793–1812.

Underglaze blue Chinese scene.

$250.00–300.00.

Coffee can and saucer (miniature).

Vienna, c. 1800–1820.

Can with loop handle, deep saucer; hand-painted rose on tan ground.

$300.00–350.00.

Coffee can and saucer (miniature).

Sevres interlaced L's with number 8, c. 1808.

Can with kicked loop handle, deep saucer; gilt scrolls on white.

$300.00 – 325.00.

Teacup and saucer.

Unidentified, possibly Old Paris.

Eggshell-thin porcelain cup with unusual square handle; scenic medallion, painted and printed flowers and birds.

$50.00 – 75.00.

Coffee cup.

Unidentified, possibly Old Paris, nineteenth century.

Straight-sided cup with ring handle; alternating panels of gilded designs; maroon, white, and band of pale yellow.

$70.00 – 80.00.

Demitasse cup and saucer.

Sampson, Emile (Paris, France), c. 1830.

Vertical fluted cup and saucer; copy of eighteenth century Dr. Wall Worcester pattern.

$300.00–400.00.

Tea bowl and saucer (miniature).

Creamware, possibly Leeds, c. 1800–1815.

Tea bowl with deep saucer; simple polychromed decoration.

$150.00–175.00.

Tea bowl and saucer.

Unmarked, English, c. 1800.

Japanese style polychromed decoration.

$150.00–200.00.

Teacup and saucer.

Wedgwood, Josiah, c. 1790.

Marriage; polished interior engine turned cup; "Acanthus" pattern saucer.

$500.00 – 600.00.

Teacup and saucer.

Wedgwood, c. 1815.

Caneware cup and deep saucer; "Prunis" pattern.

$200.00 – 225.00.

Coffee can without saucer.

Wedgwood, c. 1820.

Pale blue jasperware; putti at play.

$300.00 – 400.00.

Teacup and saucer.

Wedgwood, c. 1850 – 1860.

Straight-sided cup with loop handle; dark blue jasperware dipped on both sides; classical figures.

$350.00 – 400.00.

Coffee can, saucer missing.

Spode, Josiah, c. 1800 – 1830.

Can with double kicked loop handle; "Blue Willow" pattern.

$75.00 – 100.00.

Teacup and saucer.

Derby, c. 1800 – 1820.

London style pedestal cup; dark blue underglaze leaves and gilt grapes and vines.

$150.00 – 200.00.

Teacup and saucer.

Hilditch and Son (England), c. 1825 – 1830.

Cup in London shape, coiled handle and thumb rest; chinoiserie under-glaze dark and light blue print with vase and oversized flowers.

$90.00 – 120.00.

Teacup and saucer.

Unmarked, Hilditch-style, c. 1815 – 1830.

London shape chinoiserie light and dark blue print with woman and boy at bridge.

$80.00 – 100.00.

Teacup and saucer.

Unmarked, Hilditch-style, c. 1815 – 1830.

London shape pedestal cup; chinoiserie orange-red transfer print with multicolored over enamels of oversized flowers; man and woman along lake.

$80.00 – 100.00.

Teacup and saucer.

Unmarked, Hilditch-style, c. 1815 – 1830.

London shape cup with deep saucer; chinoiserie transfer print with polychrome over enamels of dark blue flowerpot; trailing red flowers and "amoeba" rocks on saucer.

$70.00 – 100.00.

Teacup and saucer.

Hilditch and Son, c. 1825 – 1830.

Pedestal cup with French loop handle chinoiserie print with overglaze enamels in multicolors; "Lady with Lyre" pattern.

$70.00 – 90.00.

Teacup and saucer.

Unmarked, English, c. 1815 – 1830+.

London style bone china cup; chinoiserie puce print with overglaze polychrome enamels of family group with oversized black vase and flowers.

$80.00 – 100.00.

Teacup and saucer.

Unknown English,
c. 1815 – 1830+.

London style pedestal cup
and heavy bone china saucer;
chinoiserie polychrome enamels; oversized vase, flowers,
and scrolls.

$80.00 – 100.00.

Teacup and saucer.

Unmarked, English,
c. 1815 – 1825.

London shape cup, deep
saucer; pink luster trim with
bat-printed scene.

$75.00 – 100.00.

Teacup and saucer.

Unmarked, English,
c. 1825 – 1835.

Bute cup with loop handle;
pink luster banded cup and
saucer with gray-black bat
transfer print somewhat in the
style of Adam Buck.

$60.00 – 90.00.

Teacup and saucer.

Maker unknown, English
(mark: three dots and #35
on saucer), c. 1825 – 1835.

London style pedestal cup;
pink lusterware, stylized
grapes and vines.

$60.00 – 90.00.

Teacup and saucer.

Unmarked, possibly Adams
(thought to have utilized
numerous animal prints),
c. 1825 – 1840.

London style pedestal cup; pink
luster banded cup and saucer
with purple bat print of a stag.

$60.00 – 90.00.

Coffee cup and saucer.

Unmarked,
possibly Rockingham,
c. 1825 – 1830.

Fluted cup with old English
handle; decorated with three
panels of enameled flowers,
alternated with gilt on cobalt
ground.

$150.00 – 175.00.

Teacup and saucer.

Unmarked, c. 1850.

London style cup, deep saucer; mulberry transfer of young woman with bow by sleeping Cupid, highlighted with hand-tinted decoration.

$70.00 – 90.00.

Teacup and saucer.

Unidentified, pattern no. 949, possibly Ridgway, c. 1825 – 1830.

Footed cup with ring handle; richly decorated with blue and gold; hand-painted flowers inside cup and on saucer.

$125.00 – 150.00.

Teacup and saucer.

Unknown maker, English, c. 1830 – 1840.

London style handled cup with pedestal base and deep saucer; pink lusterware of fruit with multicolored enamels.

$80.00 – 100.00.

Coffee cup and saucer.

Maker unknown, English, c. 1830–1850.

Heart-shaped molded cup and saucer, broken loop handle with upright thumb rest; pink (gold) lusterware with trailing band and green grasses and blue dot enamels.

$70.00–100.00.

Teacup and saucer.

Gaudy Welsh, maker unknown, c. 1830–1835.

Cup with high broken loop handle; "Floret" pattern.

$90.00–120.00.

Teacup and saucer.

Gaudy Welsh, c. 1860s.

Fourteen-paneled cup, ring handle with spur; panels of polychrome flowers, underglaze cobalt blue.

$90.00–120.00.

Teacup and saucer.

Unidentified, probably English,
c. 1840 – 1850.

Cup with "D" shaped, feathered handle;
hand-enameled scenes, much gilding.

$100.00 – 125.00.

Teacup and saucer.

Mason, Charles, c. 1840.

Slightly flared cup with gilt kicked loop
handle, deeply indented saucer; cobalt and
gold floral and butterflies.

$250.00 – 300.00.

Teacup and saucer.

Minton (pattern #5641),
c. 1851.

Straight-sided cup with
kicked loop handle, deep
saucer; gold scrollwork,
medallions of hand-painted
flowers.

$100.00 – 150.00.

Coffee cup and saucer.

Cauldon, c. 1860–1880.

Flared, scalloped cup with French loop handle, molded vine leaf base around four feet; flow blue decoration.

$125.00–175.00.

Demitasse cup and saucer.

Unmarked, English registry mark dated 1871.

Footed cup with loop handle, thumb rest and spur; simple molded flower design; pink ground.

$50.00–75.00.

CABINET CUPS AND SAUCERS

There is an infinite variety of cup and saucer styles for both the new and experienced collector. Highly treasured by advanced collectors are the exquisite cabinet cups and saucers made by the leading porcelain factories in Europe in the eighteenth and nineteenth century. These lovely cups and saucers were considered works of art and were proudly displayed in the estates of the nobility. They were so fine and fragile that one cannot believe that they were made for use — hence the term cabinet cup.

STYLES

Many ornamental cups and saucers were large, normally of can shape, with straight sides or a flaring rim. These cans were single or double handled, and some originally had covers with figural finials. The saucer or stand was highly decorated.

The finest artists of the time decorated the elaborate cabinet cups and saucers. The decoration, often done in compartments or richly scrolled medallions, had scenes and figures, sometimes alternating with floral bouquets. For the collector, artist signed pieces are more valuable. The subject matter also influences price. Portraits are most valuable, followed by landscapes, animals and birds, and finally fruits and flowers.

Sprigged flowers, leaves, and branches were popular on Meissen cabinet ware in the mid-eighteenth century. In the 1820s, the revival of flower-encrusted pieces lent new life to extravagant objects to fill china cabinets. A cabinet cup in Coalport's "Coalbrookdale" style would surely delight an advanced collector.

Jeweled specimens are highly regarded by collectors today. The "jewels" were made by dabbing spots of different colored enameling or richly colored glaze or gilt to simulate jewels. Sevres is credited with some of the finest jeweled cabinet cups and saucers. In England a superb example of this type of decoration was carried out at Worcester on the cabaret set made in 1865 for the Countess of Dudley. Turquoise jewels (enamels) were applied to a gold ground, creating a stunning effect. In the 1890s, Coalport created some lovely cabinet ware with gold, turquoise, and coral jeweling.

TREMBLEUSES

The trembleuse was first introduced at the French factory of St. Cloud in the early eighteenth century. This two-handled cup had a distinctive type of large saucer with a pronounced ring or rail in the middle to hold the rim of the cup securely. The French name implies that these saucers were a boom to those with trembling or shaky hands.

Examples may be found in which the central ring is elaborately pierced, so that any liquid spilled over the side could drain away into the bottom of the saucer. Similar objects, known as teacup stands, were made in silver or Sheffield plate, the central ring often being detachable.

Trembleuses were rare and choice in their own time and are more so today. The French examples were widely imitated by porcelain manufacturers in Austria, southern Germany, and England. Majolica trembleuses were made at Castelli in Italy.

CABARET SERVICES

Cabaret services, déjeuners, or tete-a-tete sets were popular in France during the third quarter of the eighteenth century. They consist of an often ornately shaped tray, small teapot, or coffee pot, milk or cream pot, a sugar, and two small cups and saucers. These lovely sets of matching porcelain were sometimes fitted into ornate boxes for use in traveling. Cabaret sets are little treasures because they are small and delicate and decorated in the richest styles.

MAKERS

SEVRES

Sevres is the luxury name in French porcelain. The earliest product, a soft-paste porcelain which was translucent and flawless, was first made in 1745 at Vincennes under the blessing of Louis XV. By the early 1800s only hard-paste porcelains were being made. The background colors were rich and exquisite. "Bleu de roi," "bleu turquoise," and "rose pompadour" were the company's most famous ground colors. The finest artists of the time decorated the elaborate cabinet cups and saucers with portraits, landscapes, and flowers.

Sevres shapes were eagerly copied in England and elsewhere. Cabinet cups were often flared, and stands had an indentation to hold the can steady. The much reproduced handle shape was a slightly "kicked loop." Needless to say, a ware so remarkable and so desired was bound to be copied. Collectors today should be aware that Sevres imitations abound.

OLD PARIS

From 1770 to the mid-1800s, many porcelain companies grew up in and around Paris. Richly decorated table services and cabinet ware were made. The porcelain is recognized by its extreme whiteness and rich gilding. Strewn flower sprigs, especially the cornflower and graceful borders, were favorite motifs, as well as landscapes and medallions of Cupids. Cup shapes were usually classical in design with elegant decoration. Although some examples were marked, many were not.

VIENNA

The Vienna Porcelain Factory, founded in 1718 by Claudius Du Paquier, was second to Meissen in producing hard-paste porcelain. From 1747 to 1784, the company's chief modeler, Johann Niedermeyer, introduced new background colors. A fine cobalt blue rivaled Sevres's "bleu roi." Today, this cobalt blue shade is still a favorite with collectors.

Richly ornamental cabinet ware was made in the neo-classical and Empire styles, often decorated with magnificent reproductions of paintings by famous artists, such as Kauffman, Rubens, and Wagner, as well as beautiful florals and elaborate gilding.

KINGS PORCELAIN MANUFACTORY (KPM)

KPM was bought and controlled by Frederick the Great in 1763, who ran the factory according to his own ideas. The mainstay of the company was a line of fine tablewares and ornamental pieces. Teaware was decorated with detailed florals, pastoral scenes, and reproductions of famous artists. Later pieces often used elaborate and sometimes excessive gilt decoration.

CAPODIMONTE

The most important and exquisite Italian porcelain was made at the Royal Palace of Capodimonte, where a factory was established in 1743 by King Charles of Naples. When Charles inherited the throne of Spain and became king in 1759, he moved the factory to Madrid. Located on the palace grounds, the new factory was called Buen Retiro. Elaborate tablewares and decorative pieces were made. The factory was moved back to Naples in 1771 and closed in 1821. All molds and models were sold to the Ginori factory at Doccia.

Contrary to popular opinion, the Capodimonte style of classical and religious figures and florals in high relief originated at Doccia. Most examples on the market today are of fairly recent manufacture.

ENGLISH COMPANIES

Beautiful cabinet cups and saucers were made by many English companies, but those made by Minton, Royal Crown Derby, Worcester, and Coalport stand out.

Minton, established in 1873, made magnificent dessert and tea services, many of which were decorated with ground colors reminiscent of Sevres with ornate gilding and extremely well-painted panels.

Royal Crown Derby was established in 1876. A most distinguished artist, Desiré Leroy, was trained at the Swiss factory and worked at Minton, before coming to Royal Crown Derby in 1890. He produced some exquisite cabinet cups and saucers, featuring birds, landscapes, fruit, flowers, and figures. Gilt embellishments were added to a rich dark blue ground.

The quality of porcelains made at Worcester during the early nineteenth century was exceptional. Cabinet pieces were richly painted and gilded. During the 1870s, magnificent porcelains in the Japanese style were produced. Jeweling was often used to enhance a border or design. In the 1920s Worcester's famous lusterwares were introduced, inspired by Wedgwood's "fairyland" and "dragon lusters."

Coalport produced a line of magnificent ornamental cups and saucers in the 1880s that are expensive and highly prized by collectors. The cups and saucers are quite small in scale, the cup measuring 55mm in diameter (excluding the handle) and saucer measuring 90mm. Frequently of the quatrefoil shape, the handles were rustic, twig, or molded as coral. Colors were often a rich cobalt blue or gold, embellished with white, gold, coral, or turquoise enameled designs and jeweling. Some had elaborately hand-painted scenic or floral reserves.

Coffee cup and saucer.

Sevres, interlaced L's, c. 1840.

Exquisitely jeweled and hand-painted reserves of birds and flowers; cobalt blue, hand gilded.

$1,000.00 – 1,500.00.

Demitasse cup and saucer.

Sevres interlaced L's mark, c. 1876.

Footed cup with high loop handle, deep saucer; scenic panel on cup, panels of flowers on saucer on blue ground.

$200.00 – 250.00.

Coffee can and saucer (miniature).

Sevres interlaced L's, c. 1850 – 1870.

Can with kicked loop handle; band of hand-painted roses on rim; floral medallion, scattered blue design on yellow ground; some wear on saucer.

$350.00 – 400.00.

Demitasse cup and saucer (possible mismatch).

Sevres, c. 1870.

Straight cup with gilt coiled loop handle; beautifully painted scene of two young boys; superbly tooled gilding on cobalt blue.

$300.00 – 400.00.

Another view of Sevres cup and saucer showing different painting on saucer.

Demitasse cup and saucer.

Limoges, c. 1890.

Quatrefoil shape; turquoise with gilt decoration.

$150.00–200.00.

Teacup and saucer.

Limoges, Klingenberg,
c. 1890–1910.

Eggshell-thin, straight-sided
cup with square gilt handle;
scenic medallion with heavy
gold leafy design.

$70.00–90.00.

Teacup and saucer.

Unidentified, marked
Claude de France,
G. Asch, Tours.

Six-fluted cup with gilt
rustic handle, gilt interior
cup; cobalt blue ground;
hand-painted goose with
crown and arrow in mouth;
saucer with raised well.

$150.00–200.00.

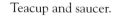

Demitasse cup and saucer.

Unmarked, Royal Vienna
style, c. 1900.

Quatrefoil cup with loop
handle; hand-painted
medallion head of young
girl; yellow with maroon
leafy design.

$60.00–75.00.

Coffee can and saucer (miniature).

Austrian enamel on silver, c. 1860–1870.

Portrait of young woman and putti; enameling also on bottom of saucer.

$600.00–700.00.

Teacup and saucer.

Austrian enamel on silver, c. 1860–1870.

Flared cup with loop handle; grapes with green translucent enameled leaves.

$1,200.00–1,500.00.

Demitasse cup and saucer.

Dresden, c. 1880s.

Lovely fluted cup and saucer with encrusted flowers outside cup and on bottom of saucer; hand-painted flowers inside.

$250.00–300.00.

Demitasse cup and saucer.

Dresden, Lamm, A., c. 1910 (Rosenthal blank).

Twelve-paneled footed cup with angular handle; cut-out of eight-petaled flower in center of cup; heavily decorated with gold enameling and jeweling.

$175.00 – 200.00.

Same Dresden cup and saucer in turquoise.

Demitasse cup and saucer.

Dresden, Lamm, A., c. 1887 – 1928 (Rosenthal blank, c. 1900 – 1907).

Footed cup with angular gilt handle; exquisite gold decoration and beading; dark red medallions with flowers and silhouette of man and woman.

$225.00 – 275.00.

Demitasse cup and saucer.

Dresden, Lamm, A., c. 1900–1907.

Cut-out of flower inside cup; alternating scenic and floral medallions.

$200.00–250.00.

Demitasse cup and saucer.

Dresden, Lamm, A., c. 1900–1907.

Garlands of beautifully painted roses on dark blue; gilt panels on white.

$200.00–250.00.

Teacup, saucer, and dessert plate.

Meissen, c. 1852–1869.

Scalloped, footed cup with ornate broken loop handle; royal blue underglaze, simple gold-bronze, "Strewn Flowers" design.

$275.00–325.00.

Teacup and saucer.

Schafer and Vater, c. 1900–1920.

Pink jasperware cup with ornate handle; two cameos of Grecian women on cup; jewels on cup and saucer.

$95.00–125.00.

Teacup and saucer.

Capodimonte style, blue crown N mark, c. 1900–1920.

Low, slightly waisted cup with twisted vine handle; beautifully hand-painted cherubs in relief.

$150.00–175.00.

Demitasse cup and saucer.

Capodimonte style, blue crown N mark, c. 1900–1920.

Tapered cup with angular kicked handle; cherubs and trees in relief, dotted gilt trim on rims.

$125.00–150.00.

Teacup and saucer.

Capodimonte style, gold crown N mark, c. 1940s.

Unusual cup on paw feet with figural dragon handle; gilt pebble design inside cup and center of saucer; cherubs in relief.

$150.00 – 175.00.

Demitasse cup and saucer.

Capodimonte style, c. 1880 – 1900.

Slightly flared and scalloped cup with divided braided handle; classical figures in relief.

$150.00 – 200.00.

Another view of Capodimonte cup and saucer. Above notice hand-painted flowers in center of saucer.

Demitasse cup and saucer.

Royal Worcester, c. 1882.

Oblong-shaped cup with unusual question mark-shaped handle; saucer straight on two sides; molded and hand-painted flowers and leaves.

$200.00 – 250.00.

Another view of Royal Worcester cup and saucer showing different decoration on back of cup.

Demitasse cup and saucer.

Copeland, c. 1810 – 1820.

Cup on molded leaf feet, ornate gilt handle; raised gold trellis work; hand-painted castle scenes.

$600.00 – 800.00.

Teacup and saucer (miniature).

Coalport, Coalbrookdale mark, c. 1825 – 1845.

Slightly scalloped molded cup and saucer, angular handle; floral encrusted with hand-painted insects.

$500.00 – 600.00.

Small demitasse cup and saucer.

Coalport, c. 1891 – 1920.

Quatrefoil shape with reinforced loop handle; gilt jeweling on rich cobalt blue.

$275.00 – 350.00.

Small demitasse cup and saucer.

Coalport, c. 1890 – 1910.

Delicately swirled and fluted cup with reinforced ring handle; coral with gilt flowers and turquoise jeweling.

$200.00 – 250.00.

Small demitasse cup and saucer.

Coalport, c. 1890–1910.

Eight-fluted cup with reinforced ring handle; gilt inside cup, handle, and decoration on cobalt.

$300.00 – 350.00.

Small demitasse cup and saucer.

Coalport, c. 1890–1910.

Straight-sided cup with loop handle; gilt inside cup, handle and stylized floral decoration on cobalt.

$300.00 – 350.00.

Small demitasse cup and saucer.

Coalport, c. 1890–1910.

Eight-fluted cup with reinforced loop handle; medallions of classical heads in white and cobalt on gilt.

$350.00 – 400.00.

Demitasse cup and saucer.

Coalport, c. 1891–1939.

Cup and saucer molded in the form of six shells; gilded handle molded as coral; gilt coral decoration.

$150.00–200.00.

Coffee can and saucer (miniature).

Coalport, c. 1881–1890.

Can (36mm high) with reinforced ring handle, deep saucer (61mm diameter); scenic medallion on gilt ground.

$300.00–350.00.

Demitasse cup and saucer.

Coalport, c. 1905.

Ornate sterling silver holder; panels of hand-painted flowers on dark red and gilt.

$125.00–175.00.

Demitasse cup and saucer.

Doulton, c. 1891–1902.

Burslem hourglass-shaped cup; hand-painted ducks, artist signed Samuel Wilson; gold jeweling.

$150.00–200.00.

Demitasse cup and saucer.

Doulton Burslem, c. 1884–1890.

Scalloped and blown-out cup with molded, ribbed band on rim; floral design.

$125.00–150.00.

Small teacup and saucer.

Royal Doulton, c. 1930–1959.

Slightly fluted, gold loop handle; gilded designs on yellow ground; gilt inside cup.

$100.00–125.00.

Teacup and saucer.

Wedgwood, c. 1920s.

Tapered cup with slight French loop handle; hummingbird luster; blue and gold.

$150.00 – 175.00.

Teacup and saucer.

Ceramic Art Co., c. 1900.

Belleek commemorative cup; double portraits "See the Players Well Bestowed"; small enameled pink flowers on border.

$200.00 – 250.00.

Teacup and saucer.

Lenox China, c. 1906 – 1924.

Low cup with geometric handle; hand-painted roses with gilt star design on saucer.

$100.00 – 125.00.

Demitasse cup and saucer.

Lenox China, c. 1952–1954.

Tapered cup with gilt loop handle; hand-painted blue jay, signed J. Nosek.

$100.00–125.00.

Demitasse cup and saucer.

Lenox for Marshall Field & Co., c. 1906–1930.

Quatrefoil shape with broken loop handle; transfer of Cupid, hand-painted clouds.

$75.00–100.00.

Coffee cup and saucer.

Stouffer Studio, c. 1906–1914.

Rounded cup with gilt flattened loop handle; hand-painted pink flowers with band of gold on rim; artist signed A. Piron.

$100.00–125.00.

Teacup and saucer.

Japanese cloisonne, c. 1920s.

Goldstone; butterflies and flowers; turquoise interior.

$250.00 – 300.00.

Chocolate cup and saucer.

Lenox, c. 1920 – 1930.

Six-paneled cup and saucer with narrow loop handle; silver overlay flowers.

$175.00 – 225.00.

Demitasse cup and saucer.

W.T. Copeland, c. 1875 – 1890.

Ribbed cup with loop handle; exquisite white jewels on cobalt blue panels; gilt flowers with coral jewel centers.

$200.00 – 250.00.

ELEGANT DINNERWARE SERVICES

Cups and saucers from the elegant dinnerware services of the late nineteenth and twentieth centuries provide much variety and offer good value for the collector.

MEISSEN

The first matching dinnerware sets were made by the Meissen Company in Germany in the 1720s. The best known and most copied porcelain decoration created by Meissen was the "blue onion" pattern. Designed in the early 1700s, it was based on a Chinese pattern from the Ming Dynasty and got its name from a stylized peach that resembled an onion. More than sixty European and Oriental companies used this decoration, and many cup and saucer collectors hunt for examples of the different "onion" styles.

Flowers were used copiously in Meissen dinnerware. In 1745, the company used German flowers painted after nature, and these floral patterns are still being used today. Meissen cups and saucers are highly prized and sought after by collectors the world over. When you pick up a piece, you can see the beauty and feel the quality of this hand-painted, finely decorated porcelain.

DRESDEN DECORATING STUDIOS

Between 1850 and 1914 as many as 200 decorating studios evolved in and around Dresden, Germany, creating a "Dresden" style, a mixture of Meissen and Vienna. Some of the decorators produced a quality of dinnerware services to match or even outdo Meissen. A popular decorating style was a simple painting of lifelike flowers on a pure white background. Meissen blanks in the Royal Flute or Quatrefoil shape were often used.

LORENZ HUTSCHENREUTHER

Lorenz Hutschenreuther established the first china factory in Selb, Germany, in 1857. While the early German factories, such as Meissen and KPM, produced porcelain for the courts and noblemen, private factories such as Hutschenreuther made china available to the general public. Many dinnerware sets were richly decorated in underglaze cobalt blue, embellished with gold and platinum. One of their most well known patterns was the "blue onion."

ROSENTHAL

Also located in Selb, Germany, is the Rosenthal factory. Phillip Rosenthal got his start by buying white ware blanks from Hutschenreuther, decorating them and selling them door to door. He opened his factory in 1879. The high quality workmanship and simplicity of design made Rosenthal's dinnerware highly acclaimed. Famous patterns include "Donatello," "Moss Rose," and "Maria."

RS PRUSSIA

The porcelain dinnerware manufactured by the Schlegelmilch brothers in Suhl and Silesia in the 1860s is especially treasured today. The RS Prussia molds are some of the most fascinating aspects of this porcelain. Many are ornately formed with scroll work, delicate flowers, or other shapes as part of the mold. Decoration was usually transfer designs with hand-applied gold enameling. Lovely soft pastel background colors were used with satiny, pearlized, or glossy finishes. Unusual molded handles can be found on cups, such as the question mark and curved loop. Popular themes include floral, animal, portrait, and scenic.

OLD IVORY

Old Ivory dinnerware was made during the late 1800s in several factories in Silesia, Germany. It gets its name from the background color of the china. The pieces are usually marked with a tiny blue fleur-de-lis/crown, as well as pattern numbers stamped on the bottom. Floral designs include orchids, roses of many colors, lavender, and holly — all on a soft, creamy background. Cups often have ornate handles in unusual shapes.

LIMOGES, FRANCE

The most popular dinnerware in the mid to late nineteenth century was Limoges porcelain. Limoges was the center of hard-paste porcelain production in France, and many companies exported lovely dinnerware, dessert, and beverage services to America. The Haviland Company, organized in 1840, was one of the most famous, and their elegant dinner services graced the White House dining room tables for many years in the nineteenth century. As many as 60,000 chinaware patterns were designed by Haviland.

Cups and saucers from dinnerware and demitasse sets in and around Limoges, France, are eagerly collected because they offer a tremendous variety of shapes and decoration and are usually very affordable. Even the blanks are interesting; many have scrollwork, beading, scalloped borders, or fancy handles. Collectors look for the hand-painted examples, preferably by French factories. Floral decor, especially the rose, is the most frequent decoration, followed by fruit themes. Some cups and saucers have deep, vivid colors, while others, especially by Theodore Haviland, have delicate pastel coloring. Many are prized because of their rich gold embellishments.

Hot chocolate was a popular beverage and is still served today in pastry shops in France. Many Limoges companies produced exquisite chocolate sets, and some collectors specialize in the gracefully shaped chocolate cups and saucers.

ROYAL COPENHAGEN PORCELAIN FACTORY

The Royal Copenhagen Factory was established in 1775, and its famous three wavy line trademark symbolizes the Sound, the Great Belt, and the Little Belt of Denmark. Along with figures and Christmas plates, their specialty was dinnerware. The most famous, ordered by Catherine the Great of Russia in 1790, was called "Flora Danica." Each piece was hand-shaped and cut and hand decorated with a native plant of Denmark. The Latin name of each flower is on the reverse of the plate or cup. "Flora Danica" is still being produced today, and the prices for it are very high. It takes the company two years to complete an order, and customers can look through a catalog and choose which Danish flowers they prefer.

MORITZ FISCHER

Moritz Fischer established a porcelain factory in 1839 at Herend, Hungary. High quality dinnerware was produced in the style of Meissen and Sevres. Many pieces were hand decorated and reticulated. They are still producing exquisite dinnerware today. Patterns are never discontinued, so it is always possible to order replacements.

ENGLISH TABLEWARES

Many English companies have produced beautiful dinnerware services. Royal Crown Derby's "Imari" pattern is richly gilded and decorated in the reds and blues of Japanese Imari ware. Minton produced exquisite hand-painted ring handle and butterfly handled teacups prized by collectors. Cups and saucers made by Royal Worcester, Wedgwood, and Coalport are eagerly collected as well.

ROYAL DOULTON

The Doulton Company created some of the most beautiful dinnerware services in their Burslem factory in the late nineteenth century. At the Chicago Exhibition in 1893 they exhibited floral painted dessert and beverage services that took some of the highest awards — the most given to any ceramic firm.

Many of the cups and saucers from the early tea, coffee, and chocolate services had the Spanish ware technique. This was the painting of very finely raised 22k gold outline traceries of flowers and leaves, combined with on-glaze enamel painting, often on an ivory or vellum ground. Many cups had elaborate gilded scroll handles.

WILLOW

Willow is the most popular tableware pattern ever made. The first was put on English porcelain in 1780 at the Caughley Pottery. Thomas Minton, one of their decorators, adapted the design from Oriental wares. The colors vary from a fine old blue to an almost purple shade. Black and even multicolored "willow" ware may be found, but the pattern is basically the same — the mandarin's pagoda, the willow tree, the bridge and run-away lovers crossing it, the boat that took them to their island, and the clouds they turned into. Over 200 different English firms, as well as potteries in continental Europe, the United States, and in Japan produced this pattern. One of the most famous producers of the ware was Josiah Spode in the early 1800s.

IRISH BELLEEK

David McBirney and Robert Armstrong founded the Belleek Pottery Company in County Fermanagh, Ireland, in 1857. Using local clay deposits, they soon produced Belleek parian china which was extremely thin and light with a creamy ivory surface and pearl-like luster. Today the dinnerware is still hand crafted, just as it was more than 100 years ago. "Shamrock," "Tridacna," "Neptune," and "Mask" are but a few of the eagerly collected teaware patterns, the "Shamrock" being the most popular.

AMERICAN BELLEEK

In the United States cups and saucers in American Belleek are of exceptional quality and sure to please the most discriminating collector. From 1883 until 1930, several potteries located in New Jersey and Ohio manufactured a type of china similar to the famous Irish Belleek parian. This luxury tableware is considered the highest achievement of the American porcelain industry.

LENOX, INC.

Today Lenox, Inc. is the only one of the companies manufacturing American Belleek still in existence, and it is the leader of American dinnerware production. With a small amount of money, Walter Scott Lenox and three partners founded the Ceramic Art Company in May 1889. It was Lenox's dream to produce an American porcelain as fine as any made in the world, and to achieve this new departure in American ceramics, Lenox hired a talented staff of decorators and artists from all over the world. This combination of artistic effort allowed beautiful works of art to be produced that today are valued by collectors.

The early pieces were highly ornate with naturalistic themes, such as seashells, marine life, applied flowers, and twig handles. The early wares were designed in the aesthetic style with raised gold and pastel matte colors. Monks, hunting scenes, flowers, and beautiful women were favorite subjects decorating the elegant tableware.

In 1906 the name changed to Lenox, Inc. to reflect Walter Scott Lenox's sole ownership of the firm, and the marks changed to show the new name. The new creative director, Frank Holmes, decided to make tableware out of their distinctive ivory Belleek body, using contemporary designs. The next major development was in 1917 when the first lithographed pattern, "Ming," was introduced. With this decal decoration Lenox could offer high quality tableware to a larger audience at lower prices. In 1918 President Woodrow Wilson selected their china to be used in the White House. After this exciting commission, a new period was begun, and soon the entire factory was devoted to tableware.

PICKARD, INC.

Pickard, Inc. was a decorating firm established in Edgerton, Illinois, in 1894. The company bought china blanks, mainly from European firms, such as Limoges, and decorated the pieces with fruits, florals, birds, portraits, and scenes. Gold-encrusted and gold-etched china was introduced in 1911 and became Pickard's most popular lines. In 1915 they introduced a line of 23k gold over a dainty floral-etched ground design. In 1938, they developed a formula for fine porcelain and began producing their own. They are now located in Antioch, Illinois.

AMATEUR PAINTING

Since about 1870 china painting was a popular hobby for many American women because the decoration of beautiful objects for the home was considered an appropriate activity for women. Much of the blank white ware came from the porcelain factories in the Limoges area of France and from Bavaria, Germany. A number of these amateur decorated cups and saucers are found in the marketplace and usually aren't as valuable as pieces decorated by factory artists.

JAPAN

Japan produced lovely Nippon beverage sets during the period from 1891 to 1921 in a variety of shapes, designs, and decorations. Much of the porcelain was hand painted with gold embellishments and beading and is enthusiastically collected today.

The Noritaki Company, founded in 1904 in Nagoya, Japan, has devoted itself to making elegant china for dining room tables around the world. Even today the company is constantly refining its technologies and innovating new chinaware.

Commonly found in the market place today are many lovely cups and saucers from Japan. Some of these are hand painted with a pastel luster finish. The cups often have a pedestal base and are on a reticulated saucer. These cups and saucers are relatively low in price and make an attractive collection.

Teacup and saucer.

Meissen, c. 1900.

Royal Flute style cup with twisted handle; "Blue Onion" pattern with crossed swords as part of design.

$125.00 – 150.00.

Coffee cup and saucer.

Meissen, c. 1900.

Scalloped and footed cup in deep saucer, ornate handle; "Blue Onion" pattern.

$125.00 – 150.00.

Demitasse cup and saucer.

Dresden, Heufel & Co., c. 1891.

Scalloped and footed cup; hand-painted flowers with band of floral and gold decoration.

$100.00 – 125.00.

Demitasse cup and saucer.

Dresden, Heufel & Co., c. 1891.

Pedestal cup; hand-painted flowers inside cup; rim of cobalt blue with gold trim and beading.

$125.00 – 150.00.

Demitasse cup and saucer.

Dresden, Klemm Richard mark, c. 1888 – 1916.

Straight-sided cup with square handle with gilt dots; hand-painted scenes alternating with florals on maroon.

$125.00 – 175.00.

Teacup and saucer.

Dresden, Klemm, Richard, c. 1886 – 1916.

Quatrefoil cup and saucer, kicked loop handle with thumb rest; alternating scenic and floral medallions on yellow and white.

$100.00 – 125.00.

Teacup and saucer.

Dresden, Hirsch, F.,
c. 1901 – 1930.

Round cup with loop handle;
hand-painted alternating
scenic and floral medallions
on pink and white.

$90.00 – 115.00.

Demitasse cup and saucer.

Dresden, Wolfsohn, Helena,
c. 1886.

Straight-sided cup with
square handle; hand-painted
floral garlands.

$75.00 – 100.00.

Demitasse cup and saucer.

Dresden, c. 1886.

Royal Flute shape with divided
feather handle; deep saucer;
hand-painted roses and gold trim.

$125.00 – 150.00.

Teacup and saucer.

Dresden, Donath, P.,
c. 1880 – 1895.

Royal Flute cup with deep
saucer; divided feathered
handle with gold dots; hand-
painted flowers.

$125.00 – 150.00.

Demitasse cup and saucer.

Unidentified gold overglaze
floral mark, possibly Dresden.

Twelve-ribbed cup and saucer;
unusual iridescent blue-green
with gold wash inside cup.

$40.00 – 50.00.

Teacup and saucer.

Dresden, Hirsch, c. 1901 –
1930.

Swirled cup and saucer, slightly
kicked loop handle; molded
flower on cup; lovely hand-
painted flowers.

$125.00 – 150.00.

Teacup, saucer, and dessert plate.

Hutschenreuther, c. 1950–1963.

Round pedestal cup with angular loop handle; cobalt blue with white flowers outlined in gold, gold leaves and stems.

$50.00–75.00.

Chocolate cup and saucer.

Rosenthal, c. 1910.

Scalloped rim and base of cup with twig handle; mixed delicate floral decoration.

$40.00–50.00.

Teacup and saucer (miniature).

Unmarked, RS Prussia mold, c. 1870–1900.

Lovely molded cup with leafy feet; metallic pinkish purple with gold inside cup.

$125.00–150.00.

Teacup and saucer.

Old Ivory, Silesia, c. 1890s.

Footed cup with interesting handle; pattern #15.

$60.00 – 75.00.

Demitasse cup and saucer.

KPM
(Royal Porcelain Manufactory), c. 1920.

Plain style cup with loop handle; hand-painted butterflies and flowers.

$100.00 – 125.00.

Coffee cup and saucer.

von Schierholz, c. 1910 – 1920.

Royal Flute cup with divided branch handle; hand-painted roses.

$75.00 – 95.00.

Demitasse cup and saucer.

Victoria Porcelain Factory, c. 1891–1918.

Quatrefoil cup with fine ribs on bottom third; plain gold loop handle; pale pink shaded to white; transfer of Cupids.

$35.00–45.00.

Demitasse cup and saucer.

Victoria Porcelain Factory, c. 1891–1918.

Swirled and fluted cup and saucer with loop handle; hand-painted flowers; worn gilding on handle.

$35.00–45.00.

Demitasse cup and saucer.

Unmarked, probably German, c. 1890.

Delicate molded cup and saucer; violet with white interior.

$35.00–40.00.

Demitasse cup and saucer.

Unmarked, probably Bavarian.

Very ornate relief molded cup on four gold feet; heavy gilt and beads.

$20.00–25.00.

Demitasse cup and saucer.

Unmarked, probably Bavarian.

Relief molded cup on four gold feet; unusual spurred loop handle; ribbed saucer; cross-hatch design.

$20.00–25.00.

Demitasse cup and saucer.

Unmarked, impressed number, probably Bavarian, c. 1900–1930.

Octagon-shaped cup with four feet; unusual handle; gold and white luster with relief molded and beaded floral design.

$30.00–40.00.

Demitasse cup and saucer.

Zeh, Scherzer & Co., Bavarian, c. 1900.

Molded and ribbed cup and saucer; rustic handle; pink flower transfer.

$30.00 – 40.00.

Demitasse cup and saucer.

K. Steinmann Co., Silesia, c. 1900.

Bulbous-shaped cup with angular handle; pastel floral transfer.

$30.00 – 40.00.

Tea and biscuit or sandwich set.

Schumann made expressly for Ovington Brothers, c. 1930s.

Transfer of Dresden style flowers.

$75.00 – 95.00.

Demitasse cup and saucer.

Johann Seltmann, c. 1950s.

Plain cup with loop handle; gold decoration on dark red.

$15.00 – 20.00.

Teacup and saucer.

Donath, P., Silesian Porcelain Factory, c. 1896 – 1922.

Royal Flute cup with divided leaf handle, deep saucer; hand-painted flowers.

$75.00 – 95.00.

Teacup, saucer, and dessert plate.

Rosenthal, c. 1908 – 1948.

Twelve-paneled footed cup with angular gilt handle; "Maria" pattern, matte finish, pearlized inside cup.

$75.00 – 90.00.

Tea and biscuit set.

Reinhold Schlegelmilch (R.S. Germany), c. 1904–1938.

Rounded "puffed out" cup with unusual handle; lovely hand-painted white flowers.

$65.00–80.00.

Demitasse cup and saucer.

Beehive mark, c. 1880–1920.

Straight-sided cup, loop handle with thumb rest; colorful Japanese decoration on bright orange ground.

$125.00–150.00.

Coffee can and saucer.

Beehive mark with Austria, probably Josef Riedl, c. 1895–1918.

Can with loop handle, worn gilding; decal decoration of putti.

$50.00–65.00.

Chocolate cup and saucer.

Beehive mark with Austria, probably Josef Riedl, c. 1895–1918.

Flared cup with scalloped bottom, ornate gilt handle; classical transfers; beaded and gilded hand decoration.

$50.00–65.00.

Coffee can and saucer.

Beehive mark, Austria, c. 1890–1918.

Can with square handle; transfer panel of mythological scene on pink; hand gilded.

$50.00–65.00.

Demitasse cup and saucer.

MZ Austria (Moritz Zdekauer), c. 1900.

Eight-paneled flared cup with awkwardly high angular handle; all gold.

$25.00–30.00.

Demitasse cup and saucer.

Unknown company in Schlaggenwald, Czechoslovakia, c. 1930–present.

Footed cup with angular handle; floral transfer.

$25.00–30.00.

Teacup and saucer.

Theodore Haviland, NY, c. 1930s.

Footed cup with gilt ring handle; "Mosaic" pattern.

$30.00–40.00.

Teacup, saucer, and dessert plate.

Theodore Haviland & Co., Limoges, c. 1904–1920.

Low cup with slightly lobed base; mixed decoration, delicate pastel flowers on white, gold trim.

$60.00–75.00.

Demitasse cup and saucer.

Theodore Haviland, Limoges, c. 1920.

Eight-paneled cup; molded design of Aladdin lamp garlands on cream; yellow band of flowers on rim; basket of colorful flowers inside cup.

$40.00–55.00.

Teacup and saucer.

Haviland & Co., made for Wright Tyndale and Van Roden Co., Philadelphia, c. 1890.

Mixed floral decoration; burnished gold trim.

$35.00–45.00.

Demitasse cup and saucer.

Haviland, decorated by Ch. Field, c. 1920.

Straight-sided cup; cream ground, pale blue leaves, royal blue and yellow flowers; gold handles and trim.

$40.00–50.00.

Demitasse cup and saucer.

Theodore Haviland,
Limoges, c. 1904 – 1925.

Slightly flared and fluted
cup with ear-shaped handle;
mixed floral decoration.

$40.00 – 45.00.

Demitasse cup and saucer.

Theodore Haviland & Co.,
c. 1904 – 1920.

Tapered cup with gilt loop
handle; printed roses.

$30.00 – 35.00.

Demitasse cup and saucer.

Haviland & Co.
made especially for
Ovington Brothers, c. 1880.

Cup and saucer with gilded
scalloped rim, high ring handle;
vividly colored flowers on outside and inside center of cup.

$60.00 – 75.00.

Teacup and saucer.

Haviland, Limoges, made for Albert Pick and Co., c. 1893–1930.

Partially fluted cup and deep saucer; gilt broken loop handle; garland trim, pastel flowers.

$45.00–55.00.

Teacup and saucer.

Theodore Haviland, c. 1925–1945.

Rounded molded cup and saucer with broken loop handle; pastel floral decoration.

$40.00–55.00.

Café au lait cup and saucer.

Haviland, c. 1920s.

Slightly molded cup, gilt loop handle with thumb rest; scalloped saucer, pastel flowers.

$75.00–95.00.

Oversize café au lait cup and saucer.

Haviland, Limoges, c. 1876 – 1889.

Tapered cup with butterfly handle; amateur decoration of orange flowers and green leaves on upper portion; mustard-yellow glaze on lower portion.

$75.00 – 100.00.

Teacup and saucer.

Limoges, decorated by Pouyot, J., c. 1914 – 1932.

Rounded cup with gold loop handle; Art Deco design on border.

$35.00 – 45.00.

Demitasse cup and saucer.

Limoges, Pouyat, J., c. 1894.

Quatrefoil cup and saucer, twisted handle with spur; gilded flowers on pink shaded to white.

$60.00 – 75.00.

Teacup and saucer.

Limoges, T&V, c. 1910.

Slightly waisted cup with scalloped saucer; large hand-painted orange and white flowers on white, gold trim.

$40.00 – 50.00.

Demitasse cup and saucer.

Limoges, Redon, M., c. 1894.

Quatrefoil cup with molded waves on bottom; scalloped saucer; gilt flowers of pale pink shaded to white.

$65.00 – 75.00.

Demitasse cup and saucer.

Limoges, c. 1920s.

Tapered cup with gold loop handle with thumb rest; garlands of pink flowers, leafy trim on rim.

$40.00 – 55.00.

Teacup and saucer.

Limoges, Ahrenfeldt, C. made for
C. Reizenstein, Pittsburgh,
c. 1894–1930.

Rounded cup with loop handle;
band of gilt and green; flowers in
center of cup and saucer.

$45.00–55.00.

Demitasse cup and saucer.

Limoges, Ahrenfeldt, C.,
c. 1896–1905.

Delicate swirled and fluted cup
with twig handle and scalloped
saucer; printed floral design.

$40.00–50.00.

Demitasse cup and saucer.

Limoges, Lanternier, c. 1891–1914.

Delicately fluted tapered cup and
molded scalloped saucer; hand-
painted violet flowers.

$35.00–45.00.

Demitasse cup and saucer.

Limoges, D & Co.,
c. 1894 – 1900.

Lovely molded cup on three gilt feet; hand-painted pink flowers, probably amateur decorated.

$40.00 – 50.00.

Demitasse cup and saucer.

Limoges made expressly for the Bailey Banks & Biddle Co., c. 1920s.

Sixteen-paneled cup with gold bands; square handle; printed scattered flowers.

$40.00 – 50.00.

Demitasse cup and saucer.

Limoges, Laporte, Raymond, c. 1891 – 1897.

Bucket-shaped cup with gilt ring handle; deep welled saucer; heavily gilt enameled bird on branches with dragonfly on ivory.

$90.00 – 125.00.

Demitasse cup and saucer.

Limoges, Bawo & Dotter, c. 1900–1914.

Eight-paneled cup and saucer with molded beading at base; factory mixed floral decoration.

$30.00–40.00.

Demitasse cup and saucer.

Limoges, c. 1896–1905.

Four-paneled cup and saucer; tiny gilt flowers on pink and white.

$65.00–75.00.

Demitasse cup and saucer.

Limoges, Pouyat, c. 1891–1932.

Slightly flared cup with loop handle; pink rose trim.

$35.00–40.00.

Demitasse cup and saucer.

Limoges, T&V, c. 1895.

Quatrefoil cup and saucer; Japanese floral motif.

$60.00 – 70.00.

Demitasse cup and saucer.

Unidentified Limoges mark.

Delicate eight-lobed ribbed cup, the base in a molded leaf design; tiny hand-painted flowers and gold enameling; ivory and pale green.

$75.00 – 100.00.

Demitasse cup and saucer.

Limoges, Lanternier mark, c. 1895.

Slightly molded and scalloped cup and saucer; hand-painted white and blue flowers on cream.

$55.00 – 65.00.

Teacup and saucer.

Limoges, c. 1960s.

Footed cup; cobalt blue and gold.

$45.00 – 50.00.

Demitasse cup and saucer.

Limoges, Bawo & Dotter, c. 1896 – 1900.

Cup with heavy gold ear-shaped handle; pale blue swirled to white; enameled flowers.

$55.00 – 65.00.

Small demitasse cup and saucer.

Limoges, Klingenberg, c. 1880 – 1890.

Straight-sided cup and saucer in unusual molded form, ornate handle; delicate hand-painted forget-me-nots with gilded leaves and stems.

$45.00 – 60.00.

Demitasse cup and saucer.

Limoges, Vignaud, A.,
c. 1939–1980.

Coffee can with loop handle;
butterfly transfer.

$30.00–35.00.

Demitasse cup and saucer.

Limoges, T&V, c. 1892–1907.

Molded cup with ornate
handle; hand-painted pink
flowers.

$40.00–55.00.

Demitasse cup and saucer.

Limoges, GDM,
c. 1891–1900.

Straight-sided cup; feather
mold; pastel flowers.

$40.00–55.00.

Demitasse cup and saucer.

Limoges, Klingenberg, c. 1880s.

Eggshell-thin porcelain cup and saucer, square handle; enameled birds and flowers with heavily applied gold.

$50.00 – 60.00.

Teacup and saucer.

Limoges, c. 1890s.

Flared cup with ear-shaped handle, deep welled saucer; mixed floral decoration with gold accents.

$35.00 – 45.00.

Demitasse cup and saucer.

Unsigned, Limoges, dated 1894.

Quatrefoil cup and saucer, coiled loop handle; gilded flowers on pink shaded to white.

$50.00 – 65.00.

Demitasse cup and saucer.

Limoges, Bawo & Dotter, c. 1915.

Hand-painted roses, gold trim and handle, artist signed. A collector favorite!

$55.00 – 75.00.

Demitasse cup and saucer.

Limoges, T&V, c. 1894.

Eight-fluted bucket-shaped cup with ornate gilt handle; garlands of gilt flowers.

$50.00 – 65.00.

Demitasse cup and saucer.

Limoges, c. 1895 – 1925.

Delicately molded cup, scalloped on bottom with gilt rustic handle; pastel floral transfer with hand-enameled gilt flowers.

$60.00 – 75.00.

Demitasse cup and saucer.

Limoges, Redon, M., c. 1894.

Quatrefoil cup with swirls on bottom, broken loop handle with spur; scalloped saucer, gilt flowers.

$65.00 – 75.00.

Demitasse cup and saucer.

Limoges, Ahrenfeldt, Charles, c. 1894 – 1930.

Straight-sided cup with angular handle; Greek key border; mixed decoration of birds and trees.

$35.00 – 45.00.

Chocolate cup and saucer.

Limoges, Pouyat, c. 1895.

Deep well on saucer; molded hairbells and gilt holly leaves and berries.

$45.00 – 55.00.

Chocolate cup and saucer.

Limoges, Field, C. mark, c. 1920.

Molded cup with broken loop handle; purple flowers on white.

$45.00 – 55.00.

Chocolate cup and saucer.

Limoges, Laviolette, c. 1896 – 1905.

Molded and scalloped; stylized gilt and black polychromed flowers.

$40.00 – 55.00.

Covered bouillon cup and saucer.

Limoges, Lanternier, c. 1891 – 1914.

Waisted cup and saucer with gadrooned rim, scalloped saucer, broken loop handles; cover has floral knop (finial); hand-painted blue forget-me-nots.

$100.00 – 125.00.

Covered bouillon cup and saucer.

Limoges, Lanternier, c. 1891 – 1914.

Hand-painted pink roses.

$100.00 – 125.00.

Tea and biscuit set.

Limoges, c. 1895.

Ornately gilded and molded rims; unusual shaped scalloped tray; lovely hand-painted flowers, artist signed.

$150.00 – 175.00.

Demitasse cup and saucer.

Sevres, interlaced L's, c. 1880 – 1900.

Bute cup with coiled loop handle, deep saucer; hand-painted scattered flowers, gilt dots on rim of cup and saucer.

$125.00 – 175.00.

Teacup and saucer.

Maker unknown, made especially for Gilman Collamore Co., NY, c. 1870–1895.

Translucent swirled and scalloped cup and saucer with molded beading; hand-painted flowers on white, gold trim.

$50.00–75.00.

Teacup and saucer.

Sarreguemines, France, c. 1895.

Translucent low cup with divided leaf handle; hand-painted flowers and gilt enameling.

$100.00–125.00.

Demitasse cup and saucer.

Unidentified, incised "depose."

Mug-shaped cup with loop handle; cobalt blue with gilt crest marked "Anvers."

$60.00–75.00.

Demitasse cup and saucer.

Unmarked.

Tapered cup with loop handle; hand-painted fern motif.

$25.00 – 30.00.

Coffee cup and saucer.

Royal Copenhagen, c. 1965.

Tapered cup with loop handle; "Flora Danica" pattern.

$700.00 – 800.00.

Demitasse cup and saucer.

Royal Copenhagen Porcelain Factory, c. 1930s.

Bucket-shaped cup with square handle; hand-painted flowers; artist signed.

$50.00 – 75.00.

Demitasse cup and saucer.

Royal Copenhagen, c. 1950.

Osier molded edge; floral transfers.

$30.00–35.00.

Demitasse cup and saucer.

Minton, c. 1870.

Slightly tapered cup with loop handle; "Aesthetic" pattern of colorful waterbirds, trees, and flowers, turquoise highlights on white.

$75.00–100.00.

Same Minton cup with old staple repair on handle.

Demitasse cup and saucer.

Royal Worcester, made for Caldwell Co. in Philadelphia, c. 1918.

Straight-sided cup with loop handle; pink with gold leaf trim.

$40.00 – 50.00.

Demitasse cup and saucer.

Royal Worcester made for Bailey, Banks & Biddle, c. 1891.

Straight-sided cup with reinforced ring handle; hand-painted flowers and butterflies on yellow.

$75.00 – 100.00.

Demitasse cup and saucer.

Royal Worcester, c. 1885.

Straight-sided cup with reinforced ring handle; brown printed floral border.

$35.00 – 40.00.

Demitasse cup and saucer.

Royal Worcester, c. 1885.

Straight-sided cup with reinforced ring handle; yellow printed transfer.

$35.00 – 40.00.

Demitasse cup and saucer.

Coalport, c. 1891 – 1939.

Flared, scalloped cup with old English handle; ornamental "Bat Wing" pattern.

$75.00 – 95.00.

Teacup and saucer.

Doulton Burslem, c. 1884 – 1890.

Fluted and ribbed cup with loop handle; hand-painted flowers in Spanish ware technique.

$125.00 – 150.00.

Teacup and saucer.

Royal Doulton, c. 1920s.

Ribbed cup and saucer, gilt loop handle; gilt jeweled decoration.

$75.00 – 100.00.

Teacup and saucer.

Doulton Burslem, c. 1884 – 1890.

Twelve-fluted and ribbed cup with loop handle; mixed decoration; colorful flowers and unusual geometric and floral border.

$125.00 – 175.00.

Teacup and saucer.

Doulton Burslem, c. 1884 – 1890.

Tapered cup with loop handle; turquoise with Japanese style gold enameled flowers.

$100.00 – 125.00.

Chocolate cup and saucer.

Doulton Burslem, c. 1891–1902.

Molded brown and cream flowers, deeply indented saucer.

$100.00–125.00.

Teacup and saucer.

Doulton Burslem, c. 1884–1890.

Cup with divided feathered handle; hand-painted stylized flowers and birds with brushed gold highlights; Japanese style.

$100.00–125.00.

Small teacup and saucer.

Doulton Burslem, c. 1891–1902.

Twelve-fluted and ribbed cup with loop handle; hand-painted flowers.

$125.00–150.00.

Demitasse cup and saucer mismatch.

Doulton Burslem, c. 1891–1902.

Hour glass-shaped cup with rose transfers. Saucer is ribbed and molded with hand-painted flowers in Spanish ware technique and is dated c. 1884–1890.

$50.00–60.00.

Teacup and saucer.

Doulton Burslem, c. 1891–1902.

Slightly flared cup with feathered loop handle; Japanese polychrome floral design.

$100.00–125.00.

Teacup and saucer.

Royal Doulton, c. 1910.

Red, black, and gold Japanese Imari-type design, gold band on rim.

$75.00–100.00.

Demitasse cup and saucer.

Unmarked, possibly Spode,
English Registry mark, c. 1889.

Cup with twenty vertical flutes with
loop handle; unusual flat saucer; blue
and white Japanese pattern.

$50.00 – 75.00.

Teacup and saucer.

Adams, c. 1898.

Straight-sided cup with loop handle;
dark blue dipped jasperware; two
Muses and Cupid in wreath on one
side; children on other.

$100.00 – 125.00.

Demitasse cup and saucer.

John Maddock & Sons, c. 1880s.

Bute-shaped earthenware cup with
ring handle; blue and white Oriental
scene.

$25.00 – 35.00.

Demitasse cup and saucer.

Unidentified mark, c. 1880s.

Porriger cup with loop handle; flow blue leafy pattern with gold veins.

$60.00 – 75.00.

Demitasse cup and saucer.

E.J. Bodley, c. 1880.

Ribbed coffee can with loop handle, raised saucer. Polychrome floral design.

$60.00 – 75.00.

Teacup and saucer.

George Jones & Sons made for Ovingtons, c. 1874 – 1924.

Twelve-paneled cup and saucer, square handle; alternating gilt flowers and designs with gold beading.

$40.00 – 50.00.

Small teacup and saucer.

Hammersley, c. 1890.

Slightly flared, scalloped, and molded cup; lovely hand-painted flowers, gold accents.

$65.00 – 75.00.

Demitasse cup and saucer.

Burgess & Leigh, c. 1890s.

Spiral fluted cup and saucer; mixed floral decoration; translucent bone china.

$40.00 – 50.00.

Demitasse cup and saucer.

Copeland-Spode, c. 1891+.

Cup and saucer with 22 vertical flutes; "Dimity" pattern.

$40.00 – 55.00.

Demitasse cup and saucer.

Unidentified, English,
mark undecipherable, c. 1890.

Straight-sided cup with loop handle;
"Blue Willow" pattern.

$25.00 – 30.00.

Demitasse cup and saucer.

Aynsley, John & Sons, English
Registry mark, c. 1883.

Six-fluted cup and saucer,
incomplete circle handle; gilt
and beaded decoration.

$125.00 – 150.00.

Demitasse cup and saucer.

Aynsley, John & Sons, c. 1883.

Six-fluted cup and saucer;
hand-painted flowers and gilt
leaves.

$100.00 – 125.00.

Demitasse cup and saucer.

Aynsley, John & Sons, c. 1883.

Six-fluted footed cup and saucer; pale yellow alternating with aqua.

$100.00 – 125.00.

Demitasse cup and saucer.

Aynsley, John & Sons, English registry mark, c. 1887.

Ribbed and fluted cup and saucer, unusual square handle; gilt trim inside and outside cup rim; dark red alternating with ivory.

$75.00 – 85.00.

Demitasse cup and saucer.

Aynsley, John & Sons, c. 1887.

Ribbed and fluted cup and saucer; squared handle; gilt hand-painted flowers, pink alternating with ivory.

$80.00 – 95.00.

Teacup and saucer.

Belleek Pottery Co.,
c. 1955–1965.

Irish Belleek cup and saucer in
Celtic Low shape, D1456/1455,
cob lustre trim.

$80.00 – 100.00.

Teacup and saucer.

Belleek Pottery Co.,
unusual pink mark and
English Registry No., c. 1899.

Irish Belleek cup and saucer in
rare Echinus shape, D645;
orange handle.

$300.00 – 325.00.

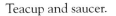

Teacup and saucer.

Belleek Pottery Co.,
c. 1891 – 1926.

Irish Belleek cup and saucer in
Erne body shape, D445; luster.

$175.00 – 225.00.

Teacup and saucer.

Belleek Pottery Co.,
c. 1891 – 1926.

Irish Belleek cup and saucer in
Erne body shape, D445; green
tint.

$175.00 – 225.00.

Coffee cup and saucer.

Belleek Pottery Co.,
c. 1891 – 1926.

Irish Belleek cup and saucer in
Fan body shape, D700; pink tint,
unusual handle.

$225.00 – 275.00.

Teacup and saucer.

Belleek Pottery Co.,
1891 – 1926.

Irish Belleek cup and saucer in
Grass body shape, D732; hand-
painted red leaves.

$225.00 – 275.00.

Teacup and saucer.

Belleek Pottery Co.,
c. 1891 – 1926.

Irish Belleek cup and saucer in
Lily body shape, D536; pink
tint.

$150.00 – 200.00.

Teacup and saucer.

Belleek Pottery Co.,
c. 1891 – 1926.

Irish Belleek cup and saucer in
Low Lily body shape, D518;
green tint.

$175.00 – 200.00.

Teacup and saucer.

Belleek Pottery Co.,
c. 1891 – 1926.

Irish Belleek cup and saucer in
Hexagon body shape, D391;
green tint; divided twig handle.

$175.00 – 200.00.

Coffee cup and saucer.

Belleek Pottery Co.,
1926–1946.

Irish Belleek cup and saucer in
Mask body shape, D1476,
D1478; luster.

$100.00–150.00.

Coffee cup and saucer.

Belleek Pottery Co.,
1891–1926.

Irish Belleek cup and saucer in
Neptune body shape, D420;
brown tint with gold trim.

$125.00–175.00.

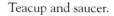

Teacup and saucer.

Belleek Pottery Co.,
1891–1926.

Irish Belleek cup and saucer in
Neptune body shape, D414;
green tint.

$150.00–200.00.

Bouillon cup and saucer.

Belleek Pottery Co.,
1891 – 1926.

Irish Belleek cup and saucer in
Shamrock and Basketweave
body shape, D1317.

$100.00 – 125.00.

Teacup and saucer.

Belleek Pottery Co.,
1863 – 1890.

Irish Belleek cup and saucer in
Thistle body shape, D779.

$275.00 – 325.00.

Coffee cup and saucer.

Belleek Pottery Co.,
1891 – 1926.

Irish Belleek cup and saucer in
Tridacna body shape, D462.

$125.00 – 150.00.

Teacup and saucer.

Belleek Pottery Co.,
c. 1891 – 1926.

Irish Belleek cup and saucer in
Tridacna body shape, D454;
pink tint.

$150.00 – 200.00.

Teacup and saucer.

Belleek Pottery Co.,
c. 1891 – 1926.

Irish Belleek cup and saucer in
Tridacna body design.

$125.00 – 150.00.

Teacup and saucer.

Belleek Pottery Co.,
c. 1955 – 1965.

Irish Belleek cup and saucer in
Harp Shamrock body design.

$80.00 – 100.00.

Teacup and saucer.

Belleek Pottery Co.,
c. 1965 – 1980.

Tall Irish Belleek cup and
saucer in Shamrock body
design.

$60.00 – 75.00.

Demitasse cup and saucer.

Ott & Brewer, c. 1880.

American Belleek four-
paneled cup with decorated
loop handle; pink luster
interior.

$100.00 – 125.00.

Coffee cup and saucer.

Ott & Brewer, c. 1863 – 1892.

American Belleek cup and
saucer in Tridacna body shape;
gold on rim and handle.

$150.00 – 200.00.

Teacup and saucer.

Ott & Brewer, c. 1863–1892.

American Belleek cup and saucer in Tridacna body shape; gold on rim and handle.

$150.00–200.00.

Demitasse cup and saucer.

Ott & Brewer, c. 1878–1892.

American Belleek cup and saucer in Tridacna body design; divided ring handle with gilt scrolls; pale pink ground.

$125.00–175.00.

Demitasse cup and saucer.

Willets, c. 1895–1909.

Belleek ribbed footed cup with dragon handle.

$75.00–100.00.

Coffee cup and saucer.

Willets, c. 1878 – 1909.

American Belleek cup and saucer in Cactus body shape; gold edges and divided gilt twig handle.

$150.00 – 200.00.

Bouillon cup and saucer.

Willets, c. 1878 – 1909.

American Belleek cup and saucer in Tridacna pattern #163, hand-painted florals and gold medallion in bottom of cup.

$225.00 – 275.00.

Teacup and saucer.

Willets, c. 1879 – 1909.

American Belleek cup and saucer in Tridacna body design; divided ring handle with gilt scrolls.

$125.00 – 150.00.

Teacup and saucer.

Ceramic Art Company (Lenox), c. 1896–1904.

American Belleek cup and saucer in Tridacna body shape, luster interior.

$150.00–200.00.

Demitasse cup and saucer.

Lenox, Inc., c. 1906–1924.

American Belleek cup with angular handle; applied sterling silver floral decoration.

$150.00–175.00.

Coffee cup and saucer.

Lenox, Inc., c. 1920s.

Ribbed footed cup with square handle; "Lenox Rose" pattern designed by Frank Holmes.

$75.00–100.00.

Demitasse cup and saucer.

Lenox, Inc., c. 1940s.

"Shell" pattern cup and saucer, ivory.

$35.00–45.00.

Demitasse cup and saucer.

Lenox, Inc., reproduction of first Lenox piece designed in 1889, limited edition.

Belleek cup and saucer in Hawthorne body shape.

$35.00–45.00.

Teacup and saucer.

Lenox, Inc., c. 1960s.

Footed cup, kicked French loop handle; "Rock Garden."

$35.00–45.00.

Demitasse cup and saucer.

Maker unknown,
made especially for Ovington's,
New York, c. 1920s.

Footed cup with square handle;
bands of heavily enameled
gold.

$40.00 – 50.00.

Coffee cup and saucer.

Rookwood, c. 1923+.

Octagonal cup with square
handle; "Blue Ship" pattern.

$100.00 – 125.00.

Demitasse cup and saucer.

Unmarked but attributed to
Russel Wright, c. 1950s.

Squatty waisted cup with loop
handle, aqua.

$20.00 – 25.00.

Demitasse cup and saucer.

Sascha Brastoff, c. 1950–1970.

Tapered coffee can with loop handle; Eskimo face attributed to Matthew Adams.

$50.00–75.00.

Demitasse cup and saucer.

Sebring Pottery Co., c. 1930.

Twenty-ribbed cup and saucer in Golden Maize style; floral transfer on yellow; crazed.

$10.00–15.00.

Demitasse cup and saucer.

Unmarked, made especially for Gilman & Collamore, New York, c. 1920s.

Straight-sided cup with unusual gold and black handle; mixed decoration of birds in tree.

$60.00–70.00.

Demitasse cup and saucer.

Chinese export,
Rose Medallion, c. 1890.

Straight-sided cup with loop
handle; medallions of figures
alternating with flowers,
birds, and butterflies.

$40.00 – 50.00.

Teacup and saucer.

Chinese, c. 1930s.

Rounded cup with loop handle;
marked "Rose Canton."

$25.00 – 35.00.

Teacup and saucer.

Nippon, c. 1891 – 1921.

Moriage "Dragonware"
motif.

$35.00 – 40.00.

Demitasse cup and saucer.

Noritaki, red M in wreath mark, c. 1911+.

Straight-sided cup with rein-forced gilt loop handle; gilt birds and flowers on orange luster; Greek key design on rim.

$25.00 – 30.00.

Teacup and saucer.

Noritaki, c. 1920s.

Plain cup with loop handle; orange luster with hand-painted scenes.

$30.00 – 40.00.

Teacup and saucer.

Japanese Satsuma, c. 1900 – 1930.

Low cup with heavy gilt loop handle with thumb rest; enameled scenes and figures.

$60.00 – 90.00.

Demitasse cup and saucer.

Occupied Japan,
c. 1945 – 1952.

Footed cup with gilt loop handle; hand-painted roses.

$20.00 – 25.00.

Demitasse cup and saucer.

Occupied Japan,
c. 1945 – 1952.

Eggshell-thin cup and saucer with angular handle; heavily enameled peacock and flowers.

$15.00 – 20.00.

Teacup and saucer.

Soko China, Japan, c. 1920s.

Low cup with fat angular handle; cobalt blue with hand-painted prunis leaves.

$30.00 – 40.00.

Demitasse cup and saucer.

Lefton China, c. 1948–1953.

Coffee can with loop handle; flowers in chintz style.

$20.00–25.00.

Teacup and saucer.

Royal Crown, Japan, c. 1950s.

Low cup with ribbed foot, open-work saucer; floral luster.

$20.00–25.00.

Demitasse cup and saucer.

Made in Japan label, c. 1950s.

Ribbed cup with broken loop handle; metallic gold.

$5.00–10.00.

Demitasse cup and saucer.

Unmarked, probably Japan.

Four-lobed cup with flared rim and molded loop handle; printed floral design.

$10.00 – 15.00.

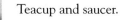

Teacup and saucer.

Shafford, Japan, c. 1950+.

Footed cup, loop handle with thumb rest, scalloped saucer; hand-painted roosters on blue luster.

$30.00 – 40.00.

Demitasse cup and saucer.

Japanese mark, c. 1920s.

Eggshell-thin lithophane cup with hand-painted scene; loop handle with large inner spur.

$25.00 – 35.00.

Teacup and saucer.

Unmarked, probably Japan, c. 1950s+.

Pedestal cup with reticulated saucer. Luster with gold decoration.

$20.00 – 30.00.

Teacup and saucer.

Unmarked, probably Japan, c. 1950s+.

Pedestal cup with reticulated saucer; luster with pink and gold design.

$20.00 – 30.00.

Teacup and saucer.

Fan Crest Fine China, Japan, c. 1950+.

Pedestal cup with ornate gilt handle; reticulated saucer; hand-painted flowers.

$25.00 – 30.00.

ENGLISH
CUPS AND SAUCERS
OF THE TWENTIETH CENTURY

Tea is the national drink of Great Britain with over 20 million cups served each day in London alone. No wonder such lavish attention and creativity have been devoted to the design of a teacup and saucer. At the center of Britain's social life, teacups have been admired and collected by many since the Dutch first brought tea to England in the early 1600s.

During the early twentieth century, many English companies produced lovely bone china dinnerware with colorful transfer decoration. Many sets were exported to the United States and Canada, and it became fashionable for young brides to collect sample cups and saucers from different sets. Today many of these bone china cups and saucers can be found in antique flea markets, shops, and shows, and prices range from $10 to $75.

A popular name in twentieth century tableware is Aynsley China. John Aynsley established a pottery in 1775 in Longton, and as tea drinking became more and more fashionable in England, he turned to tea and dessert services. By the turn of the nineteenth century, he was making them of bone china, still the present company's specialty. Their "Wild Tudor" pattern with spiral fluting remains popular today. Princess Diana selected the "Rosedale" pattern for her 1981 wedding to the Prince of Wales.

The Crown Staffordshire Porcelain Company was established in 1833 by Thomas Green and remained in the Green family until 1964. It is now part of the Wedgwood Group. The firm made a wide variety of attractive bone china table ware that is popular today, including some elaborate hand-enameled examples.

Another name frequently found on twentieth century bone china is that of Royal Grafton which is the trademark of Alfred B. Jones and Sons, 1880–1972. The firm made a wide range of fine bone china dinnerware.

Tuscan China tablewares, established by the R.H. and S.L. Plant Co. in 1898, can also be readily found today. Tea and breakfast services became the staple of the company. In 1966 they became part of the Wedgwood Group and were named Royal Tuscan in 1971. Many of their cups and saucers are characterized by large dramatic flower designs.

After World War II, the Minton Company's high quality bone china tableware was in considerable demand at home and abroad. Many new patterns were designed, including the bestselling "Haddon Hall" pattern, first designed in 1949. Old patterns were still popular, especially "Minton Rose," introduced in 1854. In 1968 Minton became part of the Royal Doulton Tableware Group. Their reputation for high quality hand painting and gilding is still retained, and many cups with beautiful ring and butterfly handles are being produced.

Royal Doulton made many stylish bone china tablewares in the 1920s and 1930s, as well as their popular line of Series Ware. These were standard bone china or pottery items, such as plates, jugs, and teaware, decorated with hand-colored transfer prints of popular themes. Examples were games, characters from legends and stories, hunting scenes, and children. They were sold as novelty wares to the general public, but bring high prices today.

Royal Worcester continues to produce tea and dinnerware, using both old traditional patterns as well as new ones. Demands for Royal Worcester porcelain were so great that a new factory opened in 1970. Much of the current decoration is still done by hand.

The Wedgwood Company continues to manufacture exceptional dinnerware services in bone china, creamware, and jasperware. During the 1960s the company acquired many English pottery companies, making them one of the largest fine china and earthenware manufacturers in the world.

A few other firms producing lovely twentieth century bone china cups and saucers that are collected today are: Adderley, Cauldon, Elizabethan Fine Bone China, Grosvenor China Ltd, Hammersley and Co., Paragon China, Rosina China Co., and Royal Albert. *The Encyclopedia of British Pottery and Porcelain Marks* by Geoffrey A. Godden is most helpful in identifying marks of these English companies.

THE SHELLEY PHENOMENON

Admired by royalty, statesmen, and thousands of brides the world over is Shelley bone china dinnerware. In 1872, Joseph Shelley became partners with James Wileman, owner of Foley China Works, thus creating Wileman & Company in Stoke-on-Trent. In 1896, the beautiful Dainty White shape was introduced. Twelve years later Wileman withdrew, and in 1925 it became known as Shelley Potteries, Ltd.

During the 1920s, many styles of cups and saucers were made, some having from six to sixteen flutes. The porcelain was so delicate, it was referred to as the "eggshell china" and established Shelley's reputation as a leading producer of quality dinnerware services. The many popular patterns were decorated with lovely pastel floral transfers. Some popular shapes were Queen Anne, Oleander, the Art Deco Vogue and Mode, and the Coupe shape introduced in 1957. In 1966 Allied English Potteries acquired control, and by 1967 the last of the exquisite Shelley dinnerware had been produced. During the last few years, the demand for Shelley cups and saucers has increased dramatically, and prices are somewhat over inflated.

CHINTZ CHINA

One of the hottest collectibles today is the charming and colorful chintz chinaware. It was first produced in the early 1900s from earthenware and bone china, continuing in production until the mid–1960s. Although copied by other countries, the chintz made in the Staffordshire factories of Royal Winton, James Kent, Crown Ducal, and Lord Nelson, during the period 1930–1960, is the most collectible today.

This cozy china is often called "wallpaper china" in the United States, "sheet transfer" or "floral" in England, and "all-over-floral" in Australia. Often worked on by young girls, lithographed sheets of gaily floral patterns were arduously fitted on to the cup and saucer so no visible joins would appear. The pattern was then sponged on and patted dry. The pattern name is usually incorporated on to the backstamp. The most coveted chintz ware was produced by Grimwades Royal Winton who designed more than 60 different chintz patterns from 1929 to the 1960s. Popular patterns are "Sweet Pea," "Anemone," "Hazel," and "Florence," and prices are skyrocketing.

SOME TIPS ON DATING ENGLISH CHINA

The use of "England" indicates a date after 1880 and usually after the 1891 U.S. Tariff Act. An absence of "England" doesn't mean the item is pre-1880 because it was only used if the manufacturer thought the item might be exported.

The words "Made in England" usually indicate a date post 1920, but some companies, such as Wedgwood and Minton, adopted it in 1910.

"Royal" appears after 1850 and is most often found in twentieth century marks. Many firms using "Royal" prefixes or trade names had no connections with royalty or royal commissions.

"Bone China" or "English Bone China" appears on twentieth century wares.

The use of "Limited" (Ltd.) after a pottery firm's name indicates a date after 1860 and usually not before 1880.

The occurrence of Rd. No. followed by a number means a date after 1884.

Demitasse cup and saucer.

Aynsley, c. 1930.

Slightly waisted and scalloped cup with gilt loop handle; band of gold enameled leaves on cobalt blue.

$35.00 – 45.00.

Coffee cup and saucer.

Aynsley, c. 1930.

Unusual corset-shaped cup with reinforced loop handle; coral ground with white band on edge; gilt design.

$30.00 – 40.00.

Teacup and saucer.

Aynsley, c. 1900–1930.

Slightly waisted cup with rein-forced loop handle; "Henley" pattern.

$40.00 – 60.00.

Teacup and saucer.

Aynsley, c. 1950s.

Swirled, fluted, and footed cup having loop handle with flat thumb rest; gilt floral band; colorful flowers in bottom of cup.

$40.00–50.00.

Demitasse cup and saucer.

Aynsley, c. 1920.

Slightly flared and scalloped cup with D-shaped handle; "Queens Garden" pattern.

$35.00–40.00.

Teacup and saucer.

Aynsley, c. 1950–present.

Scalloped pear-shaped cup with coiled handle; gilt flowers on black.

$30.00–45.00.

Demitasse cup and saucer.

Aynsley, c. 1950–present.

Coffee can with gilt loop handle; gold scrolls on turquoise, white band.

$35.00–45.00.

Demitasse cup and saucer.

Aynsley, c. 1980s.

Slightly ribbed cup with unusual handle having large flat gilded thumb rest; "Rosedale" pattern, chosen by Princess Diana for her wedding to the Prince of Wales.

$40.00–50.00.

Teacup and saucer.

Aynsley, c. 1950–present.

Spiral fluted cup and saucer, kicked loop handle; floral transfer.

$40.00–45.00.

Teacup and saucer.

Aynsley, c. 1959.

Footed cup with unusual handle; signed, "To commemorate the opening of the St. Lawrence Seaway by Her Majesty Queen Elizabeth II 1959."

$40.00 – 55.00.

Teacup and saucer.

Crown Staffordshire, English Registry mark, c. 1938.

"Maytime" pattern.

$30.00 – 40.00.

Sandwich set.

Crown Staffordshire, c. 1930 – present.

Footed cup, puffed out and ribbed waist; broken loop handle; ribbed tray; floral transfer on white.

$35.00 – 45.00.

Demitasse cup and saucer.

Crown Staffordshire, c. 1935.

Cup with loop handle; poly-chromed bird, butterflies, and flowers with scroll border.

$35.00 – 45.00.

Coffee cup, saucer, and dessert plate.

Crown Staffordshire, c. 1930s.

Scalloped white cup and saucer with printed roses.

$45.00 – 60.00.

Oversized coffee cup and saucer.

Crown Staffordshire, c. 1930s.

Amusing golf scene.

$100.00 – 125.00.

Demitasse cup and saucer.

Susie Cooper, c. 1950+.

Tapered cup with loop handle; swirled and fluted saucer; dark blue with sgraffito leaves.

$40.00 – 60.00.

Teacup, saucer, and dessert plate.

R.H. & S.L. Plant, Tuscan China, c. 1947 – 1960+.

Slightly tapered, scalloped cup with loop handle and thumb rest; lovely cherry blossom transfer.

$45.00 – 60.00.

Demitasse cup and saucer.

R.H. & S. L. Plant, Tuscan China, c. 1947+.

Scalloped cup and saucer, loop handle with thumb rest; hand-painted pansies.

$40.00 – 55.00.

Teacup and saucer.

Tuscan China, c. 1947–1960.

Gilded, footed, and slightly scalloped cup and saucer; gold floral transfer on aqua.

$30.00–40.00.

Teacup and saucer.

Tuscan China, c. 1947–1960.

Gilded, footed, and scalloped cup; "Du Barry Rose."

$30.00–40.00.

Teacup and saucer.

Tuscan China, c. 1947–1960.

Scalloped cup and saucer, coiled handle; dramatic large white flower inside cup and saucer on webbed yellow ground.

$30.00–40.00.

Coffee cup and saucer.

Tuscan China, c. 1947+.

Tapered cup with broken loop handle; scenic transfer.

$30.00 – 35.00.

Demitasse cup and saucer.

Minton, c. 1950s.

Coffee can with gilt loop handle, deep saucer. Rich hand-enameled flowers and ferns in gold on turquoise ground.

$60.00 – 75.00.

Demitasse cup and saucer.

Spode, c. 1950 – 1960.

London style cup; pate-sur-pate effect; molded white flowers on pale blue, moss roses inside cup and saucer.

$35.00 – 45.00.

Demitasse cup and saucer.

Minton, c. 1951 – present.

Swirled, fluted cup and saucer, kicked loop handle, "Ancestral" pattern.

$35.00 – 45.00.

Breakfast cup and saucer.

Royal Crown Derby, c. 1940 – 1941.

High-waisted scalloped cup (3" high, 3¾" diameter) with loop handle; artist signed; "Rosemary" pattern.

$60.00 – 75.00.

Teacup and saucer.

Royal Crown Derby, c. 1940 – 1941.

High-waisted scalloped cup with loop handle; "Rosemary" pattern; artist signed.

$60.00 – 75.00.

Bouillon cup and saucer.

Royal Crown Derby Co., made for Gilman & Collamore & Co., c. 1905.

Fine eggshell bone china cup with broken loop handles with feathered top; pink roses.

$65.00 – 75.00.

Coffee cup and saucer.

Royal Doulton, c. 1920s.

Tapered cup and saucer with loop handle; "Glamis Thistle" pattern, artist signed.

$100.00 – 125.00.

Demitasse cup and saucer.

Royal Doulton, made for Tiffany & Co., c. 1913.

Straight-sided cup with rein-forced ring handle; printed Oriental bird and trees.

$40.00 – 60.00.

Tea and biscuit set.

Royal Doulton,
c. 1950–present.

Footed cup with French loop
type handle; medallions of
roses on white.

$30.00–40.00.

Tableware group.

Royal Doulton, c. 1930s.

"Eden" and "Daffodil"
bone china patterns.

(Courtesy of Royal
Doulton UK Ltd.)

$30.00–40.00 each.

Teacup and saucer.

Wedgwood, c. 1900–1920.

Quatrefoil cup with loop
handle; slight well and
raised sides on saucer;
printed floral design.

$60.00–75.00.

Teacup and saucer.

Wedgwood, c. 1935.

Pear-shaped cup with loop handle; hand-painted flowers.

$40.00–50.00.

Teacup. (Matching saucer not shown.)

Wedgwood, c. 1950– present.

Slightly footed cup with kicked loop handle. Turquoise border, printed gargoyle design, fruits in center.

Teacup and saucer: $40.00–60.00.

Teacup and saucer.

Wedgwood, c. 1900–1920.

Quatrefoil cup; dark blue and white prunis motif.

$60.00–75.00.

Coffee can and saucer.

Wedgwood, c. 1925.

Can with deep saucer; dark blue dipped Jasperware; classical figures

$90.00 – 100.00.

Demitasse cup and saucer.

Wedgwood, c. 1945 – 1961.

Coffee can with loop handle, saucer with deep well; turquoise band of gargoyles; fruits inside saucer.

$40.00 – 60.00.

Teacup and saucer.

Wedgwood, c. 1950 – present.

Waisted cup with loop handle, ribs on rim of saucer and waist of cup. Embossed Queen's Ware.

$25.00 – 35.00.

Teacup, saucer, and dessert plate.

Coalport, c. 1945–1959.

Scalloped and footed cup and saucer, loop handle with thumb rest; "Cairo" pattern.

$60.00–80.00.

Teacup and saucer.

Coalport, c. 1945–1960.

Scalloped cup with thumb rest; "Anniversary" pattern.

$40.00–50.00.

Teacup and saucer.

Coalport, c. 1935.

Scalloped cup and saucer, coiled handle with spur; bird transfer.

$35.00–45.00.

Teacup and saucer.

Cauldon, c. 1905–1920.

Straight-sided cup with loop handle; gray-blue transfer with multicolored over-enamels and elaborate gilding.

$40.00–60.00.

Small teacup and saucer.

Cauldon, c. 1905–1920.

Pedestal footed and slightly scalloped rim with leafy design; gold divided loop handle; printed flowers.

$40.00–50.00.

Coffee cup and saucer.

Cauldon made for Gilman & Collamore, c. 1905–1920.

Flared cup on top and bottom; unusual high handle formed as a scroll; printed flowers.

$40.00–55.00.

Coffee cup and saucer.

Elizabethan Fine Bone China, c. 1964–present.

Twelve-fluted footed cup; loop handle with inner spurs; floral transfer.

$20.00–25.00.

Teacup and saucer.

Grosvenor China Ltd., c. 1960s.

Waisted, footed cup with loop handle; large turquoise band with gilt design; floral transfer inside cup and in center of saucer.

$30.00 – 40.00.

Teacup, saucer, and dessert plate.

Hammersley & Co., c. 1939–1960.

Waisted, footed cup with ring handle; transfer of grapes, nuts, autumn leaves.

$40.00–60.00.

Teacup and saucer.

Hammersley & Co.,
c. 1932–present.

Fluted cup and saucer; flower
decoration, gold accents.

$30.00–40.00.

Teacup and saucer.

Paragon China Co.,
c. 1939–1949.

Slightly scalloped, footed cup
with loop handle with thumb
rest and inner spur; bands of
dark red, cream, and white
decorated with gilt.
(Author's personal teacup.)

$40.00–60.00.

Teacup and saucer.

Paragon, c. 1932–1938.

Scalloped, flared cup and
saucer, D-shaped handle; floral
transfer inside cup and saucer;
pink ground.

$30.00–40.00.

Teacup and saucer.

Royal Albert
(Thomas C. Wild & Sons),
c. 1945+.

Eight flutes with ribbing close
to foot, broken loop handle
with thumb rest; rose transfer.

$25.00 – 35.00.

Tea and biscuit set.

Royal Albert
(Thomas C. Wild & Sons),
c. 1945+.

Eight-fluted pedestal cup on
tray; floral medallions, cobalt
blue and white.

$50.00 – 65.00.

Coffee cup and saucer.

Royal Albert, c. 1945 – present.

Six-lobed cup with question
mark handle; "Cosmos" no. 10
from Flower of the Month
series; hand painted.

$40.00 – 45.00.

Teacup and saucer.

Salisbury Crown China,
c. 1930 – 1950s.

Cup with loop handle having
thumb rest and spur; enameled
and printed flowers.

$30.00 – 40.00.

Coffee cup and saucer.

Mason's Ironstone China, Ltd.,
c. 1930s – present.

Straight-sided cup with ribbing
on rim and on edge of saucer;
"Vista" pattern.

$40.00 – 50.00.

Coffee cup and saucer.

Queen Anne (Shore &
Coggins), c. 1950 – 1966.

Footed, ribbed cup and saucer;
"Happy Anniversary"
commemorative.

$35.00 – 45.00.

Teacup and saucer.

Copeland-Spode,
c. 1891 – present.

Swirled, fluted cup and saucer,
loop handle; "Fairy Dell"
pattern.

$45.00 – 55.00.

Bouillon cup and saucer.

Foley China Works,
E. Brain & Co., c. 1890.

Shell molded and fluted two-
handled cup; pastel flowers.

$60.00 – 80.00.

Teacup and saucer.

Foley Bone China,
E. Brain & Co., c. 1945–1963.

Corset-shaped, scalloped, and
footed cup with loop handle;
flowering blackberry transfer;
pink interior cup.

$35.00 – 40.00.

Teacup and saucer.

Wileman & Co.,
Foley Potteries, c. 1892–
1910 (early Shelley).

Twelve-fluted cup with
angular gilt decorated handle;
pink and cream with delicate
gilt branches and dots.

$50.00–75.00.

Teacup and saucer.

Shelley Potteries, Ltd.,
c. 1925–1940.

Six-fluted cup and saucer with
loop handle; "Dainty Blue"
pattern.

$50.00–75.00.

Teacup and saucer.

Shelley, c. 1925–1940.

Six-fluted cup and saucer with
loop handle; "Thistle" pattern.

$50.00–75.00.

Demitasse cup and saucer.

Shelley, c. 1925–1940.

Delicately fluted and ribbed cup with loop handle; "Begonia" pattern.

$40.00–60.00.

Teacup and saucer.

Shelley, c. 1925–1940.

Scalloped cup with gilt foot and loop handle with inner spur; "Mayfair" pattern.

$50.00–75.00.

Teacup and saucer.

Shelley, c. 1925–1940.

Six-fluted cup with loop handle; turquoise polka dots.

$50.00–75.00.

Teacup and saucer.

Shelley, c. 1925–1940.

Flared and molded cup with gilt foot and handle; rose pattern inside cup; pale yellow ground.

$50.00–75.00.

Teacup and saucer.

Shelley, c. 1925–1940.

Six-fluted cup with loop handle; "Windflowers" pattern.

$50.00–75.00.

Coffee cup and saucer.

Shelley, c. 1925–1940.

Slightly flared molded cup with loop handle; colorful floral pattern.

$50.00–75.00.

Teacup and saucer.

Shelley, c. 1925 – 1940.

Fourteen-fluted cup and saucer; floral inside cup; soft blue ground.

$50.00 – 75.00.

Teacup and saucer.

Shelley, c. 1925 – 1940.

Six-fluted and ribbed rim of cup and saucer; "Campanula" pattern.

$50.00 – 75.00.

Teacup and saucer.

Shelley, c. 1925 – 1940.

Flared and gilt footed cup with high gilded loop handle; heavily gilded flowers and white leaves on rich red ground.

$50.00 – 75.00.

Demitasse cup and saucer.

Shelley, c. 1925–1940.

Six slight flutes and ribs with loop handle; floral pattern.

$40.00–60.00.

Teacup, saucer, and dessert plate.

Shelley, c. 1925–1940.

Twelve-fluted cup with angular handle; florals on pale green.

$80.00–125.00.

Teacup and saucer.

Shelley, c. 1925–1940.

Six-fluted cup and saucer; "Wild Flowers" pattern.

$50.00–75.00.

Teacup and saucer.

Shelley, c. 1925 – 1940.

Six-fluted cup with loop handle; "Begonia" pattern.

$50.00 – 75.00.

Teacup and saucer.

Shelley, c. 1940s.

Waisted, fluted cup with loop handle; "Summer Glory" chintz pattern.

$60.00 – 90.00.

Teacup and saucer.

Shelley, c. 1925 – 1940.

Corset-shaped cup with D-shaped handle; "Primrose" pattern in chintz style.

$60.00 – 90.00.

Teacup and saucer.

Grimwades, Royal Winton,
c. 1950s.

Slightly flared, footed cup with
ring handle; "Sweet Pea"
pattern in chintz style.

$140.00 – 180.00.

Teacup and saucer.

Grimwades, Royal Winton,
c. 1950s.

Slightly flared, footed cup with
loop handle; chintz "Chelsea"
pattern.

$150.00 – 200.00.

Teacup and saucer.

Crown Ducal,
A. G. Richardson & Co.,
c. 1925+.

Low cup with loop handle;
birds and flowers in chintz
style.

$45.00 – 60.00.

Teacup and saucer.

Samuel Radford, c. 1938–1957.

Flared cup with D-handle; paisley chintz style.

$40.00–60.00.

Teacup and saucer.

Crown Ducal, c. 1925+.

Low cup with angular handle; ten-sided saucer; chintz style.

$45.00–50.00.

MINIATURES

Miniatures have been made for thousands of years. Tiny toys, vases, jars, and other items have been uncovered by archeologists and explorers, and these small treasures are housed in museums throughout the world.

Little things have a fascination for everyone, and the collecting of miniatures has been a popular pastime since the eighteenth century. It is still one of the world's leading hobbies, and many cup and saucer collectors are miniature enthusiasts.

DOLLHOUSE SIZE

Dollhouse-size miniatures are the smallest — usually scaled an inch to the foot. During the late seventeenth century, miniature china dinnerware sets were produced in England and Europe to furnish miniature rooms for adults. By the nineteenth century many more companies produced these sets, and they were made for children's dollhouses, as well as those of adults.

Mary of Teck, wife of George V of Great Britain, king from 1910–1936, was an avid collector of dollhouses and miniatures. Because of her interest, the hobby regained popularity in the 1930s through the 1950s, and early dollhouse-size miniatures are now quite rare, usually housed in museums or private collections.

The most common examples of dollhouse-size cups and saucers found in the market place today date from the twentieth century. In France, several companies in the Limoges area produced them around the turn of the century. Examples of lovely molded cups with leafy feet and unusual shaped handles were manufactured by the RS Prussia Company, c. 1900. In England in the 1930s, miniature tea sets with trays, which were exact replicas of full-size sets, were made by Shelley Potteries, Crown Staffordshire Co., and Wedgwood. In the United States, Leneige Company made miniature cups and saucers in the 1930s. Beginning in 1950, miniature tea sets were mass produced in Japan and China and are still being exported today. Many of these new sets are of average to poor quality and feature floral decoration, as well as the popular "Blue Willow" and "Blue Onion" patterns.

TOY SIZE

A size of miniature, larger than the doll-house but smaller than child's size, has confused collectors and dealers alike. Miniatures in this size are often mistakenly referred to as salesman's samples.

One of England's foremost authorities on British ceramics, Geoffrey Godden, explains in his book, entitled *Guide to English Porcelain*, that the finer porcelain tea sets were not "hawked about the country as was the cheaper utilitarian pottery." Godden negates the idea that a fine miniature tea set, such as a 1765 Lowestoft example, was a salesman's sample but believes it was made and sold purely as a child's toy. He proves this by citing several cases where the patterns and shapes of the miniatures did not occur on full-size wares.

In the book, *Coalport,* by Michael Messenger, we see that miniature coffee cans (36mm high) and matching saucers (61mm in diameter) were made in the 1880s, strictly as cabinet pieces. Messenger says that there was a substantial demand for these tiny, exquisite pieces, and the Coalport Company tried to keep up with the competition.

Messenger further explains that the decoration was superbly painted by the famous artists of the time, even though they were unsigned because of their small size. The decoration was as proficient as that found on larger examples, and although the scene might be no larger than the top of a thumbnail, the painting was perfect in detail, color, and quality.

These toy-size miniatures served several purposes. First, as in the example of the Coalport coffee cans, they were merely to collect and display in a cabinet. Secondly, to serve as a method of teaching manners and social graces to children of wealthy families in the Victorian era. These teacups and saucers were frequently decorated with historical scenes and mottos. Finally, as the name implies, they could be used as toys for children to enjoy.

Imagine a Victorian nursery in England. On a small, battered wooden table by the fire, you might find a miniature tea set laid out on a finely embroidered lace tablecloth. The set might be plain white ironstone with a blue rim or a finely hand-painted one of delicate eggshell-thin porcelain. In England, as well as other countries, playing house was a favorite occupation of little girls.

These toy-size cups and saucers were made in the same forms, shapes, and styles as the full-sized ones of the period. They were manufactured as early as the sixteenth century in China and western Europe. The potters of Nuremberg, Germany, were famous for their miniature bowls, vases, and dinner services decorated in vivid colors. Early tea bowls and saucers made by Meissen occasionally turn up. Small pottery items decorated in blue and white were produced in the Netherlands in the seventeenth century and were introduced to England in the 1690s. Soon "baby house wares" were part of the normal stock of the Staffordshire potteries.

Miniature creamware, stoneware, and porcelain dishes were widely produced in the nineteenth century, and signed examples by Coalport, Minton, Spode, and Worcester are highly sought. Coffee cans made by Vienna and Sevres can be found with exquisite hand-painted scenic and floral reserves. Miniature cups and saucers, often in the popular quatrefoil shape, were decorated by the Dresden studios in the late nineteenth century. Today, Shelley miniature teawares of the twentieth century are avidly collected, and prices are usually double that of a full-sized item.

Highly prized by collectors are the rare Austrian enamels on silver. These miniature cups and saucers were made strictly as cabinet or show pieces and were exquisitely decorated, many having enameling on both the bottom of the cup or can and saucer as well. Prices for these little gems can reach over $1,000.

CHILD'S SIZE

During the Victorian era, wealthy families furnished a nursery for their children. While they partook of tea in the parlor, the children were served in the nursery. This practice required child-size tea sets. Teacups were made to hold three or four ounces, just the right size for three-year-olds and up.

This size miniature was produced in England, Germany, and the United States in the nineteenth century. Manufacturers decorated these pieces with animal themes, nursery rhymes, fairy tales, children's activities, and the artware of famous illustrators.

One of these was Kate Greenaway, an English artist, who lived from 1846–1901. She gained worldwide fame as an illustrator of children's books, and her characters were used to decorate children's dishes. It is said that she disliked to draw feet so she put her chubby curly-haired boys in long coachman's coats and her bonneted little girls into high-waisted party dresses with only the tips of their shoes showing. Her little people turned up everywhere, and many companies in Europe copied her.

Children's size miniatures are the most abundant and reasonably priced today. American production of children's ware reached a peak during World War II before the less costly Japanese ware became available.

SALESMAN'S SAMPLES

Salesman's samples are actual models made by a ceramics company. They often carried advertising messages to boost the sales of their products. They were accompanied by a carrying case, the indisputable mark of a salesman's sample. These samples were shown to wholesalers and retailers so that they could place an order for a line of tea ware. These samples are rare and highly priced.

Teacup and saucer.

Leneige, U.S., c. 1930.

Dollhouse-size cup with six flutes, footed with butterfly handle; hand-painted florals on cobalt, gilt inside cup.

$125.00 – 150.00.

Teacup and saucer.

Crown Staffordshire, c. 1930s.

Dollhouse-size cup with flared rim, orange French loop handle; printed floral decoration, green saucer.

$75.00 – 100.00.

Teacup and saucer.

Limoges, after 1891.

Dollhouse-size fluted bone china cup with loop handle; hand-painted flowers.

$100.00 – 125.00.

Coffee cup and saucer.

Wedgwood, c. 1920+.

Dollhouse-size fluted bone china cup with loop handle; hand-painted flowers.

$125.00 – 175.00.

Tea bowl and saucer.

Unmarked, late eighteenth century.

Draped ribbon design on blue ground; hand-painted urn in purple camaieu.

$300.00 – 400.00.

Teacup and saucer.

Unidentified, marked Rose Crown.

Dollhouse-size flared and low waisted cup with unusual gilt handle; hand painted.

$75.00 – 100.00.

Coffee cup and saucer.

Unmarked.

Bell-shaped cup with loop handle; hand-painted Oriental scene, heavy porcelain.

$50.00 – 75.00.

Coffee can and saucer.

Meissen, c. 1860 – 1924.

Can with loop handle, deep saucer; hand-painted flowers.

$300.00 – 350.00.

Teacup and saucer.

Meissen, c. 1860 – 1924.

Low cup with loop handle; bird painting with insects.

$300.00 – 350.00.

Teacup and saucer.

Meissen, c. 1880–1920.

Rounded cup with loop handle; hand-painted flowers.

$300.00–350.00.

Teacup and saucer.

Meissen blank, outside painting, c. 1860–1880.

Rounded cup with loop handle; Cupid in reserve in purple camaieu style on yellow ground.

$275.00–325.00.

Teacup and saucer.

Meissen blank, decorated outside, c. 1870–1895.

Rounded cup with loop handle; hand-painted scenes in Watteau style, yellow ground.

$300.00–350.00.

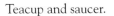

Teacup and saucer.

Dresden, Carl Thieme Porcelain Factory, c. 1888–1901.

Scalloped and fluted cup with London handle, deep saucer; alternating hand-painted scenes and flowers on dark red.

$250.00–275.00.

Teacup and saucer.

Unidentified mark, possibly Dresden, c. 1870–1895.

Rounded cup with loop handle; applied forget-me-nots outside cup and on bottom of saucer; hand-painted flowers and insects on saucer.

$250.00–300.00.

Teacup and saucer.

Dresden, Helena Wolfsohn, c. 1850–1881.

Rounded cup, loop handle with gold dots; hand-painted scenes in Watteau style.

$300.00–350.00.

Teacup and saucer.

Dresden style, c. 1870–1895.

Quatrefoil shape cup and deep saucer, loop handle; hand-painted scenes alternating with flowers.

$275.00–300.00.

Teacup and saucer.

Dresden, Helena Wolfsohn, c. 1850–1881.

Rounded cup with loop handle with gold dots; hand-painted scenes in Watteau style, floral medallions.

$325.00–375.00.

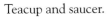

Coffee can and saucer.

Dresden, Carl Thieme Porcelain Factory, c. 1888–1901.

Can with square handle; medallion having hand-painted lighthouse and ships on blue ground.

$350.00–400.00.

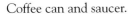

Teacup and saucer.

Brenner & Liebmann, Germany, c. 1887 – 1923.

Rounded cup with loop handle; blue and white Oriental design.

$75.00 – 100.00.

Teacup and saucer.

Unmarked, possibly R. S. Prussia, c. 1890s.

Well-molded and deeply waisted fluted cup with unusual gilt handle; hand-painted white flowers.

$100.00 – 125.00.

Coffee cup and saucer.

Elfinware, unmarked, c. 1900 – 1920.

Straight cup with loop handle, ribbed saucer trimmed with blue applied forget-me-nots; cup encrusted with moss and flowers.

$75.00 – 95.00.

Coffee can and saucer.

Beehive mark, c. 1884–1902.

Can with loop handle, deep saucer; scenic medallion on dark green, turquoise jeweled decoration.

$300.00–350.00.

Coffee cup and saucer.

Delft-style, Holland, c. 1950s.

Mug style cup with heavy loop handle; flowers in underglaze blue.

$80.00–95.00.

Teacup and saucer.

Unmarked, c. 1830–1840.

Waisted cup with London-shaped handle; gilt floral and scroll design, applied flowers.

$200.00–250.00.

Teacup and saucer.

Unidentified scrolled mark.

Slightly waisted cup with French loop handle; dark red silhouette of woman playing piano inside cup, couple dancing minuet; gilt scrolls.

$150.00 – 175.00.

Teacup and saucer.

Limoges, c. 1885.

Scalloped cup; professionally decorated.

$125.00 – 150.00.

Teacup and saucer.

Limoges, Bawo & Dotter, c. 1896 – 1900.

Quatrefoil cup attached to saucer; delicate gilded flowers, brushed gold trim.

$100.00 – 125.00.

Teacup and saucer.

Unmarked, English, c. 1850.

Flared cup, ring handle with spur; Japanese Imari design; hairline crack.

$50.00 – 75.00.

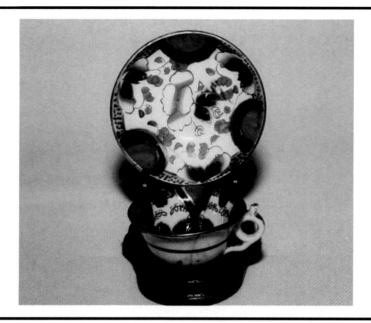

Teacup and saucer.

Edwards & Brown, Staffordshire Potteries, c. 1882 – 1910.

Footed cup with angular handle; stylized flowers on cobalt.

$150.00 – 175.00.

Coffee can and saucer.

W.M. Goss, c. 1862–1891.

Bucket-shaped can; Goss Heraldic Porcelain, "City of Edinburgh."

$100.00 – 125.00.

Teacup and saucer.

Copeland-Spode, c. 1891+.

Rounded cup with gilt loop handle; colorful hand-painted Japanese design.

$200.00 – 250.00.

Teacup and saucer.

Unmarked, probably Spode.

Waisted cup, handle with thumb rest; colorful polychromed enamels.

$150.00 – 175.00.

Teacup and saucer.

Spode, c. 1891 – 1925.

Hand-painted blue flowers with gold trim.

$125.00 – 150.00.

Teacup and saucer.

Spode, c. 1950s.

Rounded cup with loop handle; pink floral transfer.

$125.00 – 150.00.

Teacup, saucer, and dessert plate.

Wedgwood, c. 1920s.

Creamware "Noah's Arc" design by Daisy Makeig-Jones.

$275.00 – 325.00.

Teacup, saucer, and dessert plate.

Wedgwood, c. 1950s.

Bone china cup with loop handle; floral transfer.

$125.00 – 150.00.

Teacup and saucer.

Wedgwood, c. 1980.

Black basalt.

$35.00 – 45.00.

Teacup and saucer.

Royal Worcester, c. 1920.

Low cup with loop handle; floral transfer.

$100.00 – 125.00.

Teacup and saucer.

Foley China, c. 1913.

Slightly flared cup with loop handle; printed floral design.

$125.00 – 150.00.

Coffee cup and saucer.

Shelley, c. 1925 – 1940.

Straight-sided cup with loop handle; pink floral transfers.

$125.00 – 150.00.

Coffee cup and saucer.

Shelley, c. 1925 – 1940.

Straight-sided cup with loop handle; blue floral transfer.

$125.00 – 150.00.

Coffee cup and saucer.

Shelley, c. 1925 – 1940.

Straight-sided cup with loop handle; floral transfer.

$125.00 – 150.00.

Teacup and saucer.

Rosina China Co., c. 1950s.

Waisted corset-shaped cup with angular loop handle; chintz design.

$75.00 – 100.00.

Teacup and saucer.

Crown Staffordshire, c. 1920 – 1930.

Tapered cup with loop handle; floral transfer.

$100.00 – 125.00.

Teacup and saucer.

Salisbury, c. 1950s.

Slightly scalloped cup with French loop handle; floral transfer.

$100.00 – 125.00.

Teacup and saucer.

Royal Adderly, c. 1950s.

Rounded cup with loop handle; white with gold flowers.

$75.00 – 95.00.

Teacup and saucer.

Gort China, U.S., paper label.

Rounded cup with loop handle; hand-painted stylized purple flowers.

$125.00 – 150.00.

Teacup and saucer.

Unmarked.

Terra-cotta cup with angular handle; unusual pulled feather motif.

$75.00 – 95.00.

Teacup and saucer.

Austrian enamel on silver, c. 1860–1870.

Round cup with ornate handle; enamels of Cupids on outside of cup; portrait of lady sitting in park on saucer; gilt vermicelli pattern.

$600.00–700.00.

Another view of Austrian cup and saucer showing enameling on bottom of cup and saucer.

Child's teacup and saucer.

Unidentified, marked Berolina, c. 1930s.

Corset-shaped cup with rustic handle; medallion of flowers on cobalt blue.

$25.00–35.00.

FIGURALS

No cup and saucer collection is complete without a few whimsical figurals. Advanced collectors might seek a cup and saucer from Meissen's "Schneeball Service" (snowball set) first designed in 1738. This famous mayflower-encrusted cup, with its reversed saucer and birds and branches in relief, was a popular type of decoration much copied by other companies.

In France several companies in and around Paris, c. 1815–1825, made teacups in swan and shell forms. Exquisite cabinet cups were formed as flowers, leaves, and nuts.

In England in the late 1750s, Wedgwood invented a green glaze suitable for decorating tea ware in the form of fruits and vegetables. Cauliflower, pineapples, and other fancy shapes were made in plastic molds. Porcelain tulip cups were popular around 1815 and were attributed to the factories of Derby and Coalport. Each cup was formed as a blossom with six petals, and the saucer was leaf-shaped.

Majolica, an opaque tin-glazed earthenware, was introduced into England around 1850. Minton, Holdcroft, George Jones, and Wedgwood all made figurals in the form of molded leaves and vegetables. In the United States in the 1880s, Griffin, Smith and Hill of Phoenixville, Pennsylvania, developed the "Etruscan" majolica line which reflected the Victorian interest in marine and plant life. Figural dinner, tea, and coffee services were made as begonias, maple and oak leaves, ferns, vegetables, fruit, bamboo, and their famous "Shell and Seaweed" pattern. English and American majolica cups and saucers are eagerly collected and bring high prices today.

Some lovely figural cups and saucers can be found in Irish and American Belleek. Shapes were influenced by marine motifs, such as sea shells, marine plants, and animals. Handles were often shaped as a twig, bamboo, or as a coral branch.

The Royal Bayreuth Company introduced their figural line in 1885. Animals, people, fruit, and vegetables decorated dinnerware. Most abundantly produced was their tomato and lobster pieces. The famous "Devil and Cards" figurals are expensive and highly sought after today.

The Japanese developed many unique figural cups and saucers as well. Nippon made a figural tea set in the form of a tomato. A child's tea set was made consisting of a child's face molded on the teapot and small cups. Noritaki had flowers, fruits, vegetables, playing cards, and animals. Occupied Japan had elephants, tomatoes, and windmills.

Houses have always been an essential part of human life, and tea sets in the form of cottages, homes, and castles were made as early as 1750 in salt glaze by Staffordshire potteries. Today, cottage ware has become a collectible category in its own right. Teacups stylized as cozy little English cottages or huts with cone-shaped roofs made in the 1930s and 40s by Price Kensington and Beswick or marked Occupied Japan can be found. From the 1950s colorful cottage tea sets can be found marked "Made in Japan" or "Japan."

Teacup and saucer.

Griffin, Smith & Hill, c. 1878–1889.

Etruscan majolica cup and saucer in "Shell and Seaweed" pattern.

$325.00–375.00.

Teacup and saucer.

Belleek Pottery Co., c. 1897–1926.

Irish Belleek cup and saucer in Neptune body design; shell feet and coral handle; green and cream.

$150.00–175.00.

Demitasse cup and saucer.

Willets Belleek, c. 1890s.

Exquisite shell-shaped cup on two gold shell feet; hand-painted flowers and gold embellishment.

$125.00–175.00.

Teacup and saucer.

Unmarked, probably Royal Bayreuth, c. 1900.

Figural cup in the form of a plump strawberry; leaf-shaped figural saucer.

$125.00 – 150.00.

Chocolate cup and saucer.

Unmarked, attributed to Royal Bayreuth, c. 1900.

Figural cup and saucer in shape of strawberry.

$200.00 – 250.00.

Demitasse cup and saucer.

Royal Bayreuth, c. 1900.

Apple-shaped cup.

$225.00 – 250.00.

Demitasse cup and saucer.

Royal Bayreuth, c. 1900.

Tomato-shaped cup.

$75.00 – 85.00.

Demitasse cup and saucer.

Unmarked, Royal Bayreuth, c. 1900.

"Devil and Cards" figural.

$200.00 – 250.00.

Demitasse cup and saucer.

Unmarked, made in Italy.

Cup and saucer in the shape of a rose; earthenware.

$35.00 – 45.00.

Demitasse cup and saucer.

Unmarked, probably made in Japan.

Figural cup and saucer in the shape of a strawberry.

$40.00 – 55.00.

Small demitasse cup and saucer.

Unmarked, attributed to Royal Bayreuth, c. 1900s.

Cup in figure of strawberry, gilt twig handle, gold wash inside cup; saucer leafy shape.

$75.00 – 100.00.

USEFUL INFORMATION

Collectors throughout the world appreciate the unique features of cups and saucers, not only because of their place in history, but because they offer such a diversity in style, shape, and decoration. Cups and saucers are relatively inexpensive; they are often beautiful; and they can be used.

Most people start collecting when they are given a cup and saucer as a gift for a birthday or anniversary or one that belonged to a relative or friend. After admiring and displaying it for a period of time, it becomes evident that it needs a companion; so they look for another, and then the collection starts to grow. It becomes interesting to include the different shapes and styles and also the various sizes, such as full-sized, demitasse, or miniature.

Whether you have a large or a small collection, it can bring enjoyment to you, the knowledgeable collector. A word to the wise — buy only what you like. Many collectors starting out will buy everything in sight and later on they will say, "How did I ever buy that?" Be selective right from the start and know in which direction you want to take in your collection.

Some beginning collectors wonder why some cups and saucers are so expensive. It's the old adage that you get what you pay for. Look for fine workmanship and good detailing. Usually, the better the quality, the higher the price. It is a good idea to buy the best examples that your budget will allow.

AVAILABILITY

It's possible to find cups and saucers at garage sales, flea markets, and swap meets. Although you probably won't discover that elusive cabinet cup or early tea bowl, it is likely that you will find some attractive twentieth century English bone china examples.

Antique shows and shops are excellent places to buy cups and saucers to add to your collection. Dealers are a great source of information. It's a good idea to let the dealers at the show or local shop know what you want. Tell them to contact you if they come up with anything you collect; you aren't obligated to buy if you don't like the item.

Local auctions are another source for your consideration. A good preview is very important. Make sure you have a magnifying glass or jeweler's loupe to help you look for damages, such as hairline cracks or chips. You also have to know the auction's house rules, as each one is different. Know what the buyer's premium is. Some auctioneers will call defects if they see them; some do not. It is the buyer's responsibility to check for damages. Auctioneers may not know everything about the item up for auction; that's where knowledge and preview come in. It is also easy to get carried away with auction fever. Set a price for yourself, and stick to it.

If you buy a cup and saucer by mail order, make sure you ask the seller about return privileges. Also ask the seller about condition, and who has the responsibility for postage and insurance.

CONDITION

There are many things to look for when buying cups and saucers. As with any fine antique of value, condition is very important. Cups and saucers get a lot of use and, therefore, are very vulnerable to small chips and hairline cracks. It is impossible to remove a fine hairline crack, although a small chip may be repairable. The handle of a cup gets considerable use and is easy to get hit and cracked. Look very carefully at the handles for repairs, or if they have been reglued. Repairs to a porcelain piece are very expensive, and qualified restorers are hard to find.

Look for excessive crazing which could take away from appearance and value. Wares may craze in the kiln if the body expands or contracts at a greater rate than the glaze.

The inside of an earthenware or soft-paste cup may have become stained from tea or coffee. Some stains may be removed by soaking the piece in household bleach.

Pieces that have gilding sometimes show gilt wear. If it's excessive, it could take away from the appearance and value.

Another important factor to consider is the quality. Are the colors pleasing to the eye, and is the piece hand painted or a decal? You can determine if a piece is hand painted by looking through a magnifying glass or a jeweler's loupe. If the piece is hand painted, you will see the brush strokes. If it is a lithograph transfer, you will see many dots. Some decorators used a combination of both. If the piece is signed by the artist, it will usually be more valuable.

Be careful that the cup matches the saucer. Are the flowers and patterns the same? Are the colors identical? Are the marks and pattern numbers the same? Unfortunately, some dealers put together a "marriage," cups and saucers that do not match, and do not let the buyer know. Experience is the best teacher.

DISPLAY

Your collection will enhance the decor of your home when properly displayed. As porcelains are fragile, they are best displayed in a glass enclosed china or curio cabinet. Shadow boxes or wall sconces make attractive ways to show off a cup and saucer as well.

There are wonderful cup and saucer stands to display your collection, and they are available in a wide assortment of styles and configurations to suit your taste. An assortment of different stands can also be used to make an attractive display. The stands can be purchased at antique shows or at local gift shops and hardware stores.

Never store fine porcelains in a very hot or cold location, as any sudden change in temperature may crack the glaze or even the piece.

MARKS

There is probably no better way to thoroughly know and understand the various ceramic manufacturers than to collect cups and saucers. To help you identify the age and maker of your collection, a good marks book is a must. Examples of some helpful marks books on the market are listed in the bibliography.

EDUCATION

Many changes have taken place over the years in the materials, decoration, and designs of cups and saucers. One of the great pleasures for the collector is to study the complexity and to sort out the facts.

Study the various manufacturers and become familiar with the history of the company and the marks they used. Learn to tell the old from the new. Some companies are still making their products today. Learn how to use the marks to date the items. Of course, hands on is the best way to learn, so visit antique shops and shows and talk to the dealers. Pick up examples and compare the feel of the old with the new.

Learn to know the style and shapes of the cups and saucers. Be able to distinguish a London-shaped cup from a coffee can. Become an expert and know the difference between a loop handle and a ring handle, and collect good examples of each style. Know the most popular colors and which are the rarest to produce.

REPRODUCTIONS

There are some companies in the antique world whose marks are extremely recognizable and desired by collectors and, therefore, highly prized, but also copied. Unfortunately, there are unscrupulous people who try to dupe the public and make a quick buck. In antiques, reproductions and reproduced marks are easy ways to fool buyers.

It is usually the most expensive and desirable marks that are targeted. Some of the most copied marks are the beehive mark from the Imperial and Royal Porcelain Manufactory of Vienna, the Augustus Rex and blue crossed swords marks used by the Royal Porcelain Manufactory of Meissen, Germany, and the interlaced "L's" of the Sevres Manufactory in France. Know the person you buy from if possible. If it doesn't look or feel right, it probably isn't. When in doubt, don't buy it.

PROTECTION

As your collection grows, you should consider getting it insured. Just think what your loss would be if there were a fire or theft. Nothing will be covered if you don't have fine arts coverage added to your home owner's insurance policy. If your insurance company requires an outside appraiser, you must hire a qualified person with recognized credentials. Look in the yellow pages of your local telephone book under appraisers or antique dealers. You may also be able to get a recommendation from an antique dealer.

RECORD KEEPING

Keep track of what price you pay for each cup and saucer you buy. It will help when it comes time to sell your collection. Write a little note about your purchases after each acquisition, such as when and where purchased or who sold it to you, including historical facts such as manufacturer, age, style, and shape. Someday, as your collection grows, you'll have all the information on hand. Tape the information on the bottom of the saucer or keep a log book.

It is also a good idea to photograph your collection for insurance purposes. You may even want to show off your pictures to fellow collectors.

BIBLIOGRAPHY

Ashby, H. K. *Cocoa, Tea & Coffee*. New York, New York: Crane, Russak & Company Inc., 1977.

Bagdade, Susan and Al. *Warman's American Pottery and Porcelain*. Radnor, Pennsylvania: Wallace-Homestead Book Co., 1994.

——. *Warman's English and Continental Pottery and Porcelain*. Radnor, Pennsylvania: Wallace-Homestead Book Co., 1991.

Bergesen, Victoria. *Bergesen's Price Guide British Ceramics*. London, England: Barrie and Jenkins, 1992.

Berthoud, Michael. *A Compendium of British Cups*. Bridgnorth, Shropshire, England: Micawber Publications, 1990.

Carter, Tina M. *Teapots*. Philadelphia, Pennsylvania: Courage Books, 1995.

Davis, Howard. *Chinoiserie: Polychrome Decoration on Staffordshire Porcelain 1790–1850*. London, England: Rublicon Press, 1991.

Degenhardt, R. K. *Belleek, The Complete Collector's Guide and Illustrated Reference*. Huntington, New York: Portfolio Press, 1978, 1993.

Denker, Ellen Paul. *Lenox: Celebrating a Century of Quality*. Trenton, New Jersey: New Jersey State Museum and Lenox China Co., 1989.

Emmerson, Robin. *One for the Pot, British Teapots and Tea Drinking*. Norwich, England: Twining Teapot Gallery at Norwich Castle Museum.

Field, Rachael. *Buying Antique Pottery and Porcelain*. Radnor, Pennsylvania: Wallace-Homestead Book Co., 1987.

Gaston, Mary Frank. *The Collector's Encyclopedia of R.S. Prussia*. Paducah, Kentucky: Collector Books, 1982.

——. *The Collector's Encyclopedia of Limoge Porcelain*. Paducah, Kentucky: Collector Books, 1980.

Godden, Geoffrey. *Encyclopedia of British Pottery and Porcelain Marks*. London, England: Barrie & Jenkins, 1986, 1991.

——. *Godden's Guide to English Porcelains*. Radnor, Pennsylvania: Wallace-Homestead Book Co., 1978, 1992.

——. *Godden's Guide to European Porcelains*. London, England: Cross River Press, 1993.

Helm, Peter. "The Hilditch Porcelains, c. 1811–c. 1867." *Staffordshire Porcelains*. Geoffrey Godden, Editor. Granada Publishing, 1983.

Holt, Geraldene. *A Cup of Tea*. London, England: Pavilion Ltd., 1991.

Huxford, Sharon and Bob. *Schroeder's Antiques Price Guide*. Paducah, Kentucky: Collector Books, 1996.

——. *Illustrated World Encyclopedia, Vol. 19*. Bodley Publishing Corp., 1965.

Kovel, Ralph and Terry. *Know Your Antiques*. New York, New York: Crown Publishers, Inc., 1967.

——. *Kovels' Antiques and Collectible Price List*. New York, New York: Crown Trade Paperbacks, 1996.

——. *Kovels' New Dictionary of Marks*. New York, New York: Crown Publisher, Inc., 1986.

Mackay, James. *An Encyclopedia of Small Antiques*. New York, New York: Harper and Row, 1975.

McGrath, Wendy. "Shelley China." *Antiques & Collecting Magazine*. Chicago, Illinois: Dale K. Graham, December 1995.

Messenger, Michael. *Coalport 1795–1926*. Woodbridge, Suffolk, England: Antique Collectors Club, 1995.

Peck, Herbert. *The Book of Rookwood Pottery*. New York, New York: Bonanza Books, 1968.

Ray, Marcia. *Collectible Ceramics*. New York, New York: Crown Publishers, 1974.

Robinson, Dorothy. *Willets Shape Book/1893 Whiteware Catalogue*. Dorothy N. Robinson, 1979.

Robinson, Dorothy and Bill Feeny. *The Official Price Guide to American Pottery and Porcelain*. Orlando, Florida: House of Collectibles, Inc., 1980.

Röntgen, Robert E. *Marks on German, Bohemian & Austrian Porcelain*. Exton, Pennsylvania: Schiffer Publishing Ltd., 1981.

——. *The Book of Meissen*. Exton, Pennsylvania: Schiffer Publishing Ltd., 1984.

Sandon, Henry. *Coffee Pots and Teapots for the Collector*. New York, New York: Arco Publishing Company, Inc., 1974.

Scott, Susan. "Chintz." *Antique Trader*. Dubuque, Iowa: Antique Trader Publications, September 20, 1995.

Siegler, Ralph. *An Illustrated Guide to Irish Belleek Parian China*. Los Angeles, California: E. Jay Lease and Associates, 1969.

Smith, Michael. *The Afternoon Tea Cook*. Collier Macmillan Canada, Inc., 1986.

——. "The Lorenz Hutschenreuther Fine China Brevier." Selb, Germany: Porzellanfabriken Hutschenreuther.

——. "The Story of Minton." Stoke-on-Trent, England: Royal Doulton Tableware, Ltd., 1978.

——. *Victoria The Charms of Tea*. Compiled by the editors of *Victoria* magazine. New York, New York: The Hearst Corp., 1991.

INDEX